WOMEN WHO LEAD IN SPORTS

Presented by

Dr. Sharon H. Porter with
Laurie Governor Curtis

Foreword by

Tonia Walker

Copyright © 2024 Perfect Time SHP LLC

All rights reserved.

ISBN: 979-8-9858585-6-3

All rights reserved. No portion of this book may be reproduced, stored in a retrieval system, or transmitted in any form or by any means—electronic, mechanical, photocopy recording, scanning, or other—except for brief quotations without the prior written permission of the publisher..

For information regarding special discounts for bulk purchases or purchases by organizations, associations, and nonprofits, please contact the publisher:
Perfect Time SHP Publishing.

info@perfecttimeshp.com

www.perfecttimeshppublishing.com

DEDICATION

To the trailblazers, game-changers, and champions—on and off the field.

Your leadership inspires generations to rise, compete, and lead with courage.

This book is for you.

Contents

Laurie Governor Curtis **10**
    About Laurie Governor Curtis 16

Dasnii Curtis **17**
    About Dasnii Curtis 23

Raven Gerald **25**
    About Raven Gerald 32

Ruth M. Goehring **33**
    About Ruth M. Goehring 41

Brandy Gresham **42**
    About Brandy Gresham 49

Monique A. J. Smith **50**
    About Monique A. J. Smith 56

Dr. Jillian McNiff Villemaire **57**
    About Dr. Jillian McNiff Villemaire 61

Kathleen Dorinda Williams **62**
    About Kathleen Dorinda Williams 72

Nicole Henry **73**
    About Nicole Trotter Henry 118

Special Acknowledgment **119**
    DeLores "Dee" Green Todd 119

About the Visionary **124**

ACKNOWLEDGMENTS

To our incredible authors—your insights, experiences, and dedication have made this book a powerful testament to the strength and leadership of women in sports. Your voices inspire, empower, and pave the way for future generations.

Thank you for sharing your wisdom, passion, and commitment to the game. This book would not be possible without you.

Foreword - Tonia Walker

Lead Author - Laurie Governor Curtis

Contributing Authors

Dasnii Curtis
Raven Gerald
Ruth M. Goehring
Brandy Gresham
Nicole Henry
Monique A.J. Smith
DeLores "Dee" Green Todd
Dr. Jillian McNiff Villemaire
Kathleen Dorinda Williams

Additional Titles in the Women Who Lead Book Series

www.womenwholeadanthology.com

 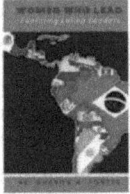   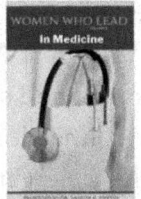

FOREWORD

By Tonia Walker

The Women Who Lead in Sports Book Collaboration gives an up close and personal testament of the trials, challenges and successes faced by females while pursuing or navigating high positions of leadership in the sports industry.

In 2018 I was blessed to co-author the book *Women Who Lead* by Sharon H. Porter where I shared the platform with 20 other powerful female leaders and had the esteem opportunity to share my story and drop a few golden nuggets from my 25 years working in intercollegiate athletics. I connected with Sharon through the bonds of the great Winston-Salem State University. Sharon is a proud alumna and I served as the institution's director of athletics. Through the connection of what we call *The Ramily*, we experienced many highs, celebrations of championships and the journey of greatness through the ties of athletics spirit and competition.

Sharon is the author and publisher of many books and is best known for her passion and exuberance for women in leadership. Her books provide a platform for women in varying disciplines to chart the path between the infancy of their careers in leadership and later career victories.

Remarkable women lead and empower others to soar, thus we must be intentional and remain committed to reach back and pull other women forward in pursuit to provide them the opportunity to grow and lead. Social scientists have calculated that a woman must be two and a half times more competent than our male counterparts to be viewed as his equal, hence we have a responsibility to develop and prepare women coming behind us to be ready to boldly step into positions of leadership.

In this latest book, *Women Who Lead in Sports,* Sharon gives a platform for women in athletics leadership to share a glimpse of their experiences as they navigate their seat at the table in a male dominated sports profession. As a female leader journeying through space in a man's world, it is important that we share our personal journeys, pour into other women, and prepare and empower them to go out and conquer the world. Through our personal testimonies, other women garner confidence, hone leadership skills and are equipped with the necessary tools for leadership.

Read this book and learn the skills necessary to carve a path toward leadership success while keeping life together and one's sanity intact. The book gives insight to what makes a good leader and why the world needs more women in leadership. It challenges women to embrace their greatness to reach their full potential, gain confidence and master the art of self-belief and overcome self-doubt. It adds tips for managing high stress situations and handling the ebbs and flows of life as a female leader in the athletics arena, all while lending secrets to achieving a healthy work-life balance. This book is a must read!

Dr. Sharon H. Porter is an educator, author, publisher, and podcast host and has dedicated much of her career to coaching, mentoring, and inspiring women at varying levels in the educational industry. She uses keen insights gathered from her relationships to coach women and help them grow in their careers.

Laurie Governor Curtis

WOMEN WHO LEAD IN SPORTS

Lead Author: Laurie Governor Curtis

Leadership: Lessons Learned on The Court

by Laurie Governor Curtis

In the ever-evolving world of sports leadership, my journey from a student athlete to the person I am today has been transformative. My story is one of passion, resilience, and an unwavering commitment to empower others.

My journey to the court started on the track. I ran track when I was in middle school. At the end of my eighth-grade year, my gym coach said that I should play basketball. I had never picked up a ball outside of the gym, but I was crazy enough to give it some thought.

Lesson #1 Learned on the court: Trust. Trust that the people who know you will see greatness and potential in you that you can't see in yourself. Believe them until you believe it yourself.

I ended up playing volleyball, basketball, and track in high school.

After my freshman year I started thinking about my next steps.. I knew I wanted to go to college but didn't know how I would afford to do it. I did well enough playing basketball in my freshman year, that I saw it as my opportunity to get to college. At that point, I put in the work, and it resulted in me earning a four-year scholarship to play at the University of Richmond.

At Richmond, I developed my leadership skills on the court. As a player, and an eventual captain, my goals were to be the best player I could be through hard work, determination, and by setting an example for my teammates. In those early years, my leadership style was one rooted in action, firmly believing that actions speak louder than words. Little did I know that these foundational experiences would become the bedrock of my future in leadership and sports.

As a speaker, author, and coach to business leaders and entrepreneurs, I found myself at the intersection of my two greatest loves - sports and leadership. I saw a need and I wanted to leverage the leadership skills I learned on the court to support other individuals and athletes off the court. From that desire, I established my own business focused on leadership development.

I learned the importance of seeing myself as more than an athlete. I have more to offer than how many points or rebounds I had in a game. It's about using the skills, discipline, grit, desire, perseverance, determination, and the resilience developed through my life experiences, to create the life that I want for myself and my family. All these things learned on the court are skills. I use to this day.

My leadership skills have evolved over the years and one of the lessons I learned on the court was the importance of self-development.

Lesson #2 Learned on the court: Self-Development. You must prepare yourself for what's ahead.

The ability to adapt to changes, be innovative, make informed decisions, and to inspire others by building a culture of learning, are benefits that come from developing oneself. As a player, I developed my basketball skills, it was just as important to develop myself personally and professionally.

No stranger to obstacles, transitioning into the world of athletics from a corporate environment, presented me with challenges. Beyond the acclimation process, I confronted a broader, pervasive challenge - the struggle to be taken seriously. Overlooked and undervalued, I rejected the notion of being deterred.

Lesson #3 Learned on the court: Tenacity. You must push through obstacles despite what it says on the clock or the scoreboard. Don't give up.

Instead, I focused on continuous self-development, engaged in clarifying conversations, and reflected on alternative strategies to overcome these obstacles. My journey as a woman in leadership is a testament to resilience, a determination to be heard, and a commitment to rewriting the narrative that surrounds women in the sports industry.

My role models in this space are my former college coach and a high school coach I coached with many years ago. Their influence fueled my steadfast belief that women can not only survive but thrive in fields where they are often told they shouldn't be.

Lesson #4 Learned on the court: Connections and Influence. Success is not accomplished alone. I could not accomplish the things that I've accomplished on and off the court by myself. It was a team effort.

These women serve as daily reminders that my aspirations are not just valid, but entirely within reach.

As a result, mentorship takes center stage in my commitment to empower and support aspiring women in sports leadership. Ongoing conversations, check-ins, and providing the space for questions and self-discovery, form the foundation of fostering an environment where individuals can navigate their journey with support and guidance.

Irrespective of gender, successful sports leadership is anchored in qualities that transcend the boundaries of the playing field.

Communication, self-awareness, leading by example, serving others, and empowering individuals, stand as the pillars of effective leadership. These qualities collectively create an environment conducive to growth, empathy, and a safe space for learning and development.

Reflecting on my journey, a standout achievement is witnessing the evolution of a team from humble beginnings to remarkable success. I take immense pride in the role my work ethic and leadership played in this transformative journey. It's a living testament to the impact one can have on a collective goal.

Staying relevant in the ever-evolving world of sports requires active networking, continuous professional development, and staying attuned to industry changes. Investing in myself through seminars, associations, and networking opportunities is not a choice but a necessity. Being visible, understanding the dynamics of the sports world, and constant growth, are vital for navigating the path to success.

For young women aspiring to take the path into sports and sports leadership, my advice is simple: understand your WHY!

Lesson #4 Learned on the Court: Clarity. Being clear about who you are (value, skills, and abilities) and what you want, and what effort you are willing to put in to get there, will allow for a clearer path towards your goal. And it is what you will hang onto when you run into challenges.

Once you understand why you want to be in sports you will be able to develop a plan to get closer to your goal. As part of the process, I recommend that you volunteer to help in various roles and expose yourself to the diverse facets of sports leadership. Get a mentor or a coach, seek guidance from others, and embrace the journey of self-discovery. Through these experiences, you'll understand your strengths, passions, and the unique contributions you can make to the world of sports leadership.

My admiration extends to female athletes and coaches who have left an indelible mark on the sports world. Their achievements, resilience, and determination inspire me to push boundaries and challenge stereotypes. Learning from their experiences adds depth to my narrative and fuels my commitment to paving the way for future generations.

Participation in sports transcends the physical realm; it builds confidence, strength, and life skills. It teaches women and girls that they are strong, fierce, and capable of conquering any challenge. The skills learned on the field – communication, teamwork, and resilience – translate into invaluable life lessons that empower women to excel in all aspects of their lives.

The current state of women in sports fills me with optimism. Pivotal moments have swung open doors once firmly closed to women. From journalism, to coaching and officiating, women are making their mark in every aspect of the sports industry. The growth is undeniable, and I am excited to be part of this transformative period.

My journey from a student athlete to a woman in sports and leadership has been a tapestry woven with passion, challenges, and achievements. It's a story of breaking barriers, overcoming, and contributing to the evolving narrative of women in sports leadership. As I continue to navigate this dynamic landscape, my hope is to inspire and pave the way for more women to follow their aspirations, redefine leadership, and leave an indelible mark on the world of sports.

About Laurie Governor Curtis

Laurie Governor Curtis is an accomplished international speaker, author, coach and consultant. She is also CEO and Founder of On The Court Solutions.

Powered by her personal experiences, Laurie helps business leaders, entrepreneurs and student athletes overcome fear, frustration and uncertainty by developing systems and strategies that propel them to new heights of success.

Her personal brand is built on a foundation of authenticity, empathy, and results-driven strategies. Laurie is a servant leader whose approach is rooted in storytelling, integrating personal experience and sharing real-life examples to achieve a heightened sense of purpose and impact.

Dasnii Curtis

WOMEN WHO LEAD IN SPORTS
Contributing Author: Dasnii Curtis

If You Are Not Uncomfortable, Then What Are You Doing?

by Dasnii Curtis

I grew up surrounded and influenced by athletics from the day I was born. My mother competed in the Olympics for track, played basketball and volleyball, and my father played football and basketball. They were both college athletes and differed in their experiences as students. When I was introduced into the world, I was also introduced to some of the most fundamental characteristics of a great human being through sports and through my parents' leadership. I watched my mother and father pour their knowledge and experiences with sports into opportunities to give back and make other people better. I will say that is one thing that drove me crazy about my parents is how busy they were with life and other people and keeping my sister and I so active. Now looking back and the way I do the same thing I can completely see the value in what they did and why they were led to do so. Their commitment to community service, even without recognition serves as fuel and has instilled some of the most wonderful core values that make me who I am today.

As a student-athlete beyond high school and college, I see the value that sports played in my parents and my life. I have always worked for everything that I set my mind to off the strength of my perseverance and discipline. I understand that my parents' willingness to make others better was not just to benefit them, but it also did something great for them. That is what fuels my desire to serve and give back. I knew this from the time I was in middle school. I always knew that I wanted to be a psychologist as it would allow me to help people. It wasn't until I started my college career at Fayetteville State University (FSU) and met my mentor that I knew that working in college athletics was my purpose.

As a student-athlete at FSU playing basketball, I was very intentional about being involved in more than just my sport. I always knew that I wanted to be more than just an athlete so that I always had something to fall back on. While I was always a talented athlete and I could produce on the court, I knew that I did not want to pursue a professional career in sports because there were so many factors that could affect how successful I was. My mentor pushed me out of my comfort zone and challenged me every day. Through doing work study with her, I was very heavily involved in learning the ins and outs of athletics. From my freshman year of doing work study and being able to help other athletes while experiencing student-athlete life myself I was captivated. I was an active member of Student-Athlete Advisory Committee (SAAC) and there were so many events and activities that allowed me to gain a love for working in athletics. The most influential part that had the biggest impact on me that drove my motivation and obsession with working with student-athletes is that my mentor was someone that spoke life in everything that I said I wanted to accomplish and put me into positions to achieve them.

One of the biggest supporters I have in my life within sports, I gained when I was in college and that relationship is something that I want to provide to my student-athletes. There were so many people in my life that told me I couldn't do this and that, but she challenged me to see beyond that and develop a whole new perspective on life and how I looked at things. I have a supportive family; however, it was that support outside of my family that encouraged and allowed me to be so effective and have such an impact in working with student-athletes. Many do not have influences that challenge them to be better, nor do they seek the opportunities on their own and so I love that I can provide some support and direction. Paying it forward is big to me and I believe that my impact and interactions with my student-athletes will allow them to not only flourish in their professional and personal lives, but also to pay that influence forward.

One of the things that has really stood out to me over the years of working in athletics is that you do not see a lot of women that work in athletics, especially with football, more specifically, of color. Throughout my career in sports, I am typically the only woman of color and that has presented some challenges. On top of that I look younger than I am so when dealing with coaches, I have had to work harder to prove that I know what I am talking about. I work in an industry that consists mainly of men. There are so many misconceptions that come along with working with men's sports as a young woman. The way I have overcome those misconceptions is by developing relationships with my players and coaches and maintaining boundaries and being very mindful of how I am representing myself. It was great having Camelia as my mentor in undergrad because before her, I did not see a woman of color in a position of power that had such an impact. It also made me aware of the importance of being able to be a support for young black men and women at Predominantly White Institutions where they can see themselves being represented and having faith that I am advocating for them in rooms with people that do not look like them. Just watching how my mentor carried herself working in a male dominated industry as a young black woman that was coming into herself and maintaining that work life balance is something I have referred to as I have been coming into myself and growing in this industry. I am in an influential position that serves not only as a mentor figure but shines light on a professional avenue that allows young black men and women that they can be in a position in athletics outside of coaching. There are several paths one can take in athletics outside of coaching.

One of my first positions was at Campbell University and I literally grinded day in and day out learning skills and the industry. It was hard getting into athletics because colleges and universities are looking for people who already have experience. I chose to pursue a master's degree after undergrad and could not find any avenues to pursue experiences working in athletics, so I am glad that I had developed a relationship with a mentor and was able to make a really good impression because if it was not for her then I would have not been able to get my foot in the door. It was very discouraging at first, but it fueled my desire even more to be just that much greater when I started off part-time at Campbell. I was definitely put to the test when I was working there, and I was able to work my way up to a full-time position. I had several women in athletics that played a major part in helping me get connected to other women and professionals in athletics and giving me the opportunity to gain the experiences. They taught me things that were above my pay grade, and I appreciate them for that because it made me into the professional that I am today. Unfortunately, after five years of being at Campbell I had a supervisor that did not see my value and it made me begin to doubt myself. I really lost my confidence because I was so invested in my career and I proved that I was competent and could advance and others saw and acknowledged how competent I was, but he couldn't see it. Through some self-work and evaluation, I realized that God was making me uncomfortable for a reason and that experience really made me reevaluate my circumstances and has played a huge part in how I carry myself today.

When you are competent and things are going really great, you can get too comfortable. So, when things get uncomfortable it is important to evaluate why and it can be for several reasons. What keeps me going when I encounter negative experiences is that things may be bad now but if you are strong enough to weather the storm there is a blessing on the other side. It differs per person, but you must have faith in the journey, and you appreciate the lessons that much more. It builds character and encourages growth so that you do not become complacent with your current situation but continue to live in your purpose and flourish. Since I am intentional in living my life with purpose it has made the quality of my experience in my professional and personal life better and I encourage others to do the same.

About Dasnii Curtis

Dasnii has been working in athletics since 2017, where she started her career part-time at Campbell University with the football program. Dasnii provided academic support and subject tutoring until she was promoted to a full-time position as Academic Advisor. She provided academic support primarily for football and oversaw the women's volleyball program as well until 2022.

After leaving Campbell University, Dasnii became the Director of Academic Success at the University of Richmond where she primarily oversaw the academic support for football and men and women's tennis.

She currently oversees the academic support program for football at Texas Tech University, in which she serves as one of the advisors and engages in academic support facilitation for offense. She also coordinates study halls. Dasnii also serves as Assistant Director of Academic Excellence at Texas Tech.

As a former basketball and cross-country student-athlete, she completed her undergraduate degree at Fayetteville State University in 2013 and earned her master's degree in Sports and Performance Psychology from the University of the Rockies in 2015.

Outside of her professional career duties, Dasnii also coached alongside her mother, Sonya Harriott, and served as Assistant Director to the Starlings- Fayetteville Volleyball Club where she served as head coach to the 18 and under, and served as the assistant coach for the 14 and under, and 12 and younger teams for two years. Now that she is currently residing in Lubbock, Texas she remains Assistant Director and provides administrative assistance and programming.

Women Who Lead In Sports

Dasnii was born in Austin, Texas and spent a great deal of her life in Fayetteville, North Carolina. Dasnii has committed her life to fulfilling her purpose in helping others through athletics. Since a young age, she has been obsessed with putting in the long hours, late nights and long weekends, tears, and sweat to optimize all opportunities to gain the experience and skills to improve the quality of life of student-athletes.

Women Who Lead In Sports

Raven Gerald

WOMEN WHO LEAD IN SPORTS

Contributing Author | Raven Gerald

The Discovery

by Raven Gerald

When we first choose to participate in a sport, it's usually for understandably selfish reasons: enjoyment, exercise, community, and a wide array of others. And for those of us whose love for the sport grows and evolves as we do, our engagement generally remains self-serving, taking on added motivations such as heightened competition, a desire for greater skill development, rewards, recognition, monetary incentives, and more.

And this "selfishness" isn't necessarily a bad thing. The journey of self-exploration that sports spark is unlike any other (*in my biased opinion*). There are few things that thrust you into the processes of character-development, relationship cultivation, and resiliency training like sports do.

When I first picked up a basketball, and every time thereafter, I did so for me.

It was fun.

It was exciting.

It was a challenge.

It gave a little girl with lots of energy, a way to expend it.

It scratched a competitive itch that I soon learned I inherently had.

It helped build a foundation of self-confidence that I *didn't* inherently have.

It forced me to crack the shell of shyness that initially "protected" me and as a result, sparked the development of lifelong personal and professional relationships.

It allowed me to experience the highs of championships, Player of the Year awards, and All-Conference honors in high school.

It led me to an NCAA Division I scholarship, a couple of conference championships, a Division II National Championship game.

Not to mention, it provided plenty of amazing trips, memorable experiences, and unique interactions over the years.

However, it also gut-punched me with a fair share of lows.

Being glued to the bench my first two years of college, I averaged less minutes per game than my grade point average (which, at the time, was also slipping lower than my little overachieving eyes had ever seen it).

I was feeling unseen, unwanted, and irrelevant, and as result, confidence was nowhere to be found.

Combine this immense feeling of failure with a diagnosis of clinical depression and anxiety, and I had the perfect recipe for internal disaster.

Meanwhile, seeking mental help wasn't the nobility it's more commonly considered to be nowadays, especially as an athlete.

So, as someone who championed honesty, I found myself telling my teammates and friends that I was going to the library when I was really visiting the campus counselor (with my hood on of course).

All while also surrendering my pride enough to accept that I needed the assistance of psychiatrist-prescribed pills to help slowly pull me out of the pit I found myself seemingly buried in.

For the first time in my life, I couldn't use any accomplishments on the court, in the classroom, or in my personal life as crutches to uphold my identity and self-worth.

I had to figure out and be comfortable with who I was at my core, the person I am with or without the "highs."

Today, I'm just as grateful for the ugly parts of this "sport-induced journey of self" as I am for the shiny ones. So, in hindsight, even the ugly parts of this journey were centered around…*me*. I first picked the ball up with myself in mind, but it wasn't until I put it down that I gradually began to realize that all the years of using basketball to better myself was so that I could one day help others do the same.

My motivation as a leader in sports is to help young people, especially young women, not only excel in their sport, but also develop the character, confidence, and transferable skills that will help them thrive *outside* of their sport as well. I want young people to be empowered to discover their God-given gifts and embrace a holistic identity. As legendary University of South Carolina Head Women's Basketball Coach, Dawn Staley calls it, I want to be a "dream merchant" for these student-athletes.

I coached for a total of eight years at the NCAA Division I, II, and III levels, and was blessed to have helped lead several amazing young women athletes during that time. While this was an incredibly rewarding experience, one of the greatest challenges I faced as a coach was the often-transactional nature of college sports. Although I was well aware of this prevalent dynamic from my time as a student-athlete, I dreamed of a way to still promote athletic success without continuing to normalize it at all costs.

Women Who Lead In Sports

While the business of sports is an undeniable reality (and is even one that we, as leaders in Athletics, benefit from), I believe that every individual's existence as a *person* must be consistently honored along with their performance as an athlete. This transformational leadership approach is the foundation to making a true and lasting impact as a coach and, in my opinion, is rooted in one simple, yet essential trait: CARE.

I truly believe, no matter how tough an athlete is required to be to effectively perform, every single one wants to feel like their leaders *care:* Care about their craft, their success, their growth, their interests, their engagement, and most simply, their presence. Everyone, athlete or not, wants to feel cared *for* and cared *about*. However, because of the uniquely consequential nature of the Athletics business, many coaches and leaders struggle to fully grasp the importance of displaying genuine, holistic care in their leadership style.

In 2022, I began to feel a nudge to step away from coaching. While I genuinely enjoyed many aspects of the work I was doing, I felt as though there was much more that I could and should be doing to positively impact collegiate student-athletes. It gradually became more and more clear that my role as a coach was not fulfilling this deeper desire and it was time for me to take a leap of faith into a different realm of Athletics.

This was a difficult pill for me to swallow, as I had spent the previous few years dedicating much of my free time toward preparing to one day become a head coach. However, this pivot away from college coaching turned out to be just what the doctor ordered.

After months of reflection, I was reminded of my "why" for coaching: Ultimately, I want to help athletes use sports as a vehicle to become the best version of themselves. My journey with mental health as a student-athlete developed a uniquely deep desire within my heart to support athletes who are trying to navigate some of the same muddy internal waters that I was. In short, I want to become who I wish I had.

Therefore, I decided to shift my focus more toward the rapidly expanding field of Sport Psychology, in which I previously earned my master's degree back in 2017. Fast forward, and at the time of this publishing, I am now one year into the Sport and Performance Psychology Doctor of Education program at the University of Western States, with an expected graduation year of 2025. Through this program, I am developing deeper knowledge and more extensive training in Applied Sport Psychology, along with a certification to become a successful Certified Mental Performance Consultant (CMPC) through the Association of Applied Sport Psychology (AASP).

As I work toward this credential and degree, I am grateful to have the opportunity to serve as a Mental Skills Coach for athletes through three different amazing organizations, as well as through my own consulting business, Undefeated Sport Psychology, which I started in March of 2023. I work in both one-to-one and team settings with athletes to help them enhance their performance by learning, developing, and applying critical mental skills such as self-talk, focus, concentration, mindfulness, goal setting, imagery, performance routines, emotion and arousal regulation, relaxation techniques, breathwork, psychological resilience, team cohesion, and more. I will also soon be pursuing clinical licensure, which will allow me to work with athletes who may be struggling specifically with mental health disorders as well.

Additionally, after months of pursuing the right position in Athletics Administration, I was recently named the Assistant Athletic Director at Trinity Washington University, an all-women's college located in Washington, D.C. I am proud to say that my growing desire to impact women student-athletes to a greater degree is transpiring in a refreshing way.

Although this part of my journey in Athletics leadership has just begun, I have no doubt that it's the right next step. Every time I put on my Performance Coach hat and sit with an athlete to help them navigate a mental block, or whenever I put on my Athletic Director hat to help develop successful systems for coaches and teams, I feel at home.

I'm excited to continue to navigate these domains and forge new pathways for women who lead in sports. Back when I was playing sports, I never could have predicted the way my career would turn out or how being an athlete would eventually impact it. But the journey to self-discovery through sports is never-ending. The more you embrace it, the better you can help others do the same.

About Raven Gerald

Raven is a Mental Skills Coach for athletes and is a Sport & Performance Psychology doctoral student at the University of Western States. She is also the Assistant Athletic Director at Trinity Washington University in Washington, D.C.

Raven earned her master's degree in Sport & Exercise Psychology from Seton Hall University in 2017 and has eight years of college basketball coaching experience to go along with over a decade of youth sports coaching experience. Prior to her coaching career, she played college basketball at the NCAA Division I & II levels, helping lead her teams to multiple championships. Additionally, Raven is a writer and mental health advocate.

Women Who Lead In Sports

Ruth M. Goehring

WOMEN WHO LEAD IN SPORTS

Contributing Author: Ruth M. Goehring

My Path to Leadership

by Ruth M. Goehring

As I attempt to assay the history of my career to best provide information and service for readers, I find it difficult to funnel my story into a meaningful and useful narrative.

Since my earliest memory, I loved sports and found I was pretty good at playing them! The sports activities available to me were simple; stickball, steam ball, stoop ball, running bases and catch. These ball games were invented by neighborhood kids to be played in the streets and backyards. No special equipment was required; just a rubber pinky ball and a cut off broomstick. Since it was the 1950s, I was only allowed to play the boy games if the team needed a substitute. Since I played better than many of the boys, I came to be picked frequently. Those days and years signify the beginning of my intolerance of gender inequities.

Fortunately for me, high school was a dream come true. I was inspired by two exceptional female physical education (PE) teachers who took me under their wings, motivating me to play organized sports and developing me into a multi-talented athlete. To this day I credit them with being the most important influences in my life. Although I was still keenly aware of gender disparities at the high school level, at the time I did not see it affecting me as a hindrance to my personal growth.

Women Who Lead In Sports

In 1964 I enrolled in State University of New York (SUNY) College at Cortland as a PE major and became a member of the intercollegiate teams. Field hockey, volleyball and basketball were the only team sports available. After four years of attendance I was a proud team member of those three team sports, having lettered in each all four years.

My academic major classes were very invigorating as well as enlightening particularly in graduate school; opening my mindset to different beliefs, attitudes and values. One particular course in sociology of sport exposed me to author Robert K. Greenleaf and his writings on the concept of servant leaders. Greenleaf is credited with starting the modern and often controversial philosophy of Servant Leadership in the 1970s. I was drawn to his idea that the relationship of leadership and service to others are intricately connected.

Tenets of his philosophy that resonate with me are listening, empathy, building community and commitment to the growth of people. Throughout my story, I will make reference to several of his tenets. If you are interested in Greenleaf's ideology, I suggest you further explore his literature.

My recollection of the five years after college when I taught physical education and coached in the public-school system was that it was a total whirlwind! I was busy, motivated, and involved in as much as I could possibly handle. Youth was on my side, but I was very short on experience. Relating to the students was gratifying, I enjoyed teaching those who were not skilled as much as those who were highly skilled. It was challenging to prepare lesson plans for activities that I myself found difficult to execute. Demonstrating some of the techniques involved in dance and gymnastics were awkwardly hilarious at times. My sense of humor was a plus for me then and the students delightfully accepted my ineptitude. Coaching was my forte and it was a humbling undertaking. Witnessing student athletes benefit from structural practices and hard work on their part morphed into successful wins in competition, was heartwarming. I was proud of their development, attitude, skills and accomplishments. The entire experience was exhilarating. I concluded my high school career satisfied that I contributed to building a community of female athletes.

It was 1973 and I moved on to Colgate University. Colgate was historically an all-male institution and was following a growing trend by transitioning to coeducational.

My responsibilities at Colgate were to develop a women's intercollegiate athlete program, coach three sports and teach in the required PE classes. Most of those classes were coeducational and posed an opportunity for me to listen to the men's thoughts and feelings about the new direction on campus. There were many negative comments, but also a select number of positive suggestions. Listening to the voices from male students was helpful in building student relationships and it broadened my approach to achieving my goals. More importantly, new laws were in place that needed to be addressed at Colgate.

"No person in the United States shall, on the basis of sex, be excluded from participation in, be denied the benefits of, or be subjected to discrimination under any educational program or activity receiving federal financial assistance."

Commonly referred to as Title IX. This is part of the Federal Civil Rights Act enacted as a section of Education amendments of 1972. It is not my intention to critique, evaluate or elaborate on the virtues of the law, but rather how reaching compliance dictated useful strategies at Colgate.

Alumni, students and several faculty were not in agreement with the reality of a coeducational campus. Certainly, the male population involved in athletics, as staff or students were apprehensive about sport budgets, sharing of facilities, loss of student athlete scholarships aid among other amenities.

The challenges facing me were obvious; how was I to build a community of acceptance and success for female athletes amid an atmosphere of conflict and resentment. My resolve was to develop a strategic management plan that would be advantageous to the men as well as the women. I clearly had empathy for the men and a sound commitment to grow the women's program to equal measure. The university supported my efforts to add field space for field hockey, develop a fair schedule for women to access the arena for basketball and volleyball, as well as adding assistant coaches for women's sports, sports medicine services, female locker rooms and need

based financial aid for female athletes. A plan was crafted to add additional intercollegiate sports and elevate club sports to a varsity level in a timely manner. I completed my tenure at Colgate after eight years. I was both pleased and proud to have had the opportunity to be a part of Colgate's initiatives and successes.

In the early 1980s opportunities for female sports leaders were expanding and I was eager to secure a position of employment whereby I could focus on administrative duties without being encumbered with coaching and teaching. In essence, I was seeking a bigger stage in athletics to develop my leadership capabilities. The University of Richmond (U of R) expressed interest in my candidacy for Coordinator of Women's Athletics. They were facing Title IX issues as well as changing their athletic profile.

At the time the Association of Intercollegiate Athletics for Women (AIAW) was the sole proprietary organization governing and sponsoring championships for women's sports from their beginning in 1972. I was impressed with the leadership among the organization, presidents, officers and membership. They were dedicated to advancing women's footprint and causes on the local and national scenes.

In 1981 when I began my tenure at U of R, the NCAA directed their attention to collegiate women's sports and established women's championships, services and membership. The AIAW was unable to remain solvent after court battles dwindled their assets. The AIAW was legally dissolved shortly after the 1981-82 academic year. The NCAA became the sole authority in operating women's athletics for its member institutions.

Westhampton College, the female coordinate college of the University, boasted a noteworthy history of success from 1914 through 1981. It was now facing a merger with Richmond College; the men's coordinate undergraduate school to compete as an NCAA Division I institution.

Westhampton alumnae were outspoken in their distaste for what was an inevitable outcome; they feared losing their identity and heritage. No longer would Westhampton be emblazoned on athletic uniforms. No longer would their future successes be identified as Westhampton College. As the newly hired Women's Coordinator of Women's Athletics, my first priority was to listen to the concerns of the current student athletes, alumnae and Deans of Westhampton. I went to great lengths to assure them that the past will always be remembered, and the future would be equally successful on a larger, more competitive level.

Additional sports were offered, facilities were upgraded, more scholarships became available, and additional coaches were hired. Services were expanded to include laundry, tutors, publicity, transportation and sports medicine among others. In addition, my role was affected as well. My title changed to Assistant Athletic Director with oversight responsibilities for both men's and women's non-revenue sports, as well as facilities and event management. Moreover, the NCAA created an avenue for women administrators to become active members within the organization. They mandated a senior woman administrator (SWA) be designated at each of its membership institutions and welcomed SWA's to serve in various capacities. This single action propelled women to have a voice within NCAA matters.

There is no doubt that the modifications made to my role at UR over the years enhanced my leadership reach beyond the athletic department to the boundaries of campus and the community. It was never a goal of mine to become a "boss". Bosses often make people anxious and fearful with their authority. I wanted to be considered a leader, helping teammates, coaches, athletes and coworkers become the best they could be. I made a multitude of mistakes along the way but was mindful to not make the same ones twice. I learned from the guidance given me and likewise learned from those who were mean spirited and confrontational. I was motivated to empower other young women in this demanding field because I believed in them, their energy and abilities. I supported and encouraged new ideas and faces in staffing and all aspects of the university community.

My entire life was athletics and my job. I was well into my late forties and an Associate Athletic Director before I valued a better balance between work and play. I began to tire of late evenings, weekends and holidays being spent on a field, arena or bleachers. I envied my coworkers who were fortunate to delegate and share responsibilities with assistants.

College athletics is supposed to be cocurricular to academics, when in reality it is a big business enterprise. Women who grew into athletic leaders through the system of player, teacher and coach now required training in business practices, finance management and legal matters in order to be successful. The focus within college athletics today has expanded to include diversity and inclusion, student-athlete leadership and development, nutrition, and psychological well-being with all requiring additional financial support. Emphasis on fundraising, endorsements, sponsorships and television revenue has affected conference affiliations with the promise of greater profit sharing and exposure. The most recent rulings on Name, Image and Likeness (NIL) involving pay for play moves college athletics toward professionalism. Restructuring of athletes transfer protocols have altered coaches recruiting techniques and team building.

There are certainly challenges that lie ahead to ensure the concept of 'student athlete' retains its core value. It is my hope and belief that this generation of female leaders will rise to the occasion and play a significant role in developing strategies to effectively move athletics to a prosperous and healthy future.

About Ruth M. Goehring

A mainstay in the University of Richmond Athletic Department for more than a quarter century, Ruth served in various roles to assist Spider student-athletes, coaches and administrators from 1981 until her retirement in 2007.

She initially served as the coordinator of Women's Athletics where she was a driving force to promote agendas for women's sports. She also was the university's Senior Woman Administrator and Associate Athletic Director for Sports, Events and Facilities.

A native New Yorker, Ruth graduated from SUNY-Cortland in 1968 where she was a four-year letter winner in field hockey, volleyball and basketball. She completed her master's degree from Cortland in 1971. Following undergraduate school, she taught physical education and coached a variety of sports in public school for five years.

Her professional collegiate career began at Colgate University where she was charged with initiating a competitive intercollegiate program as the school transitioned to co-education.

Brandy Gresham

WOMEN WHO LEAD IN SPORTS

Contributing Author: Brandy Gresham

When You Know Better You Do Better

by Brandy Gresham

As a former childhood and collegiate athlete, I have always had an undeniable love for sports. In addition to frequently being intrigued by what made people tick, think and or behave the way they did. Being an athlete has always had so many compounding layers that many do not fully comprehend. Yet, understanding that an athlete's mental health can play in their ability to athletically perform/recover, academically excel, socially engage and culturally assimilate. This is what truly inspired me to pursue a career in sports leadership.

Despite my ongoing desire to combine the study of the mind and behaviors with one's ability to athletically perform at their highest peak. I was truly unaware as to how this could be done. Back in the late 90s and early 2000s , Google did not provide a clear-cut blueprint as to how a position I envisioned *in my head* could be both obtained and lucrative.

Yet, the love of sports and psychology, I never deserted. As I have always believed that "everything is mental" and in order to be well in all areas of our lives, whether physically, emotionally, financially, athletically and spiritually, just to name a few. Our mindset(s) and mental state has to be prioritized and not "back-seated."

After working 14 years as a Clinician in the Mental Health and Substance Abuse Field, I received a call in 2018 that literally changed my life and the years that followed thereafter. Being appointed as the first Director of Student Athlete Well-Being and Mental Health Counselor at my alma mater and in the Mid-Eastern Athletic (MEAC) Conference is what brought my childhood dream to fruition. As this opportunity was now a yet another physical manifestation of what I visualized long ago.

With years of experience both athletically and clinically I was humbly confident of my ability to pursue and act as an agent of change as a leader in sports in the area of Mental Health, Wellness and Performance. I am very proud of this trailblazing accomplishment, facilitated by my ability to display my gifts, talents and "superpower." As a result of this position, I was later extended so many other opportunities, such as presenting at the 2023 Black Student Athlete Summit in Los Angeles, California and being offered an Athletic Counselor position at the University of Michigan.

Yet, in all things, pertaining to growth, change and elevation. There comes a degree of apprehension, struggle and challenges, in which I had and continue to have my share of. The indirect and or passive-aggressive minimization of the importance of my role and the services provided as a woman leader in sports. The genuine ignorance of cultural limitations and unspoken taboo pertaining to mental health and wellness. In addition to the stigmatic resistance of shedding the unproductive behaviors, mindsets and coaching styles of the "olden days" that continue to box us in from increasing the necessary "conversation" of openly and comfortably discussing the positive outcomes of addressing, improving and or maintaining one's Mental Health and Wellness.

How did I overcome some of these challenges you may ask? I simply SHOWED UP every day being ME, with a smile and all the positive energy in the world. This is what I did even when frustrated, disregarded, overlooked and or when viewed simply as a "checked box". I continued to do my job, I continued to advocate, I continued to educate, I continued to promote and provide solutions, I continued to develop genuine rapports with those I worked with, because what I did know is that we are all products of our environment and in most cases. What we do not understand, what makes us feel uncomfortable and or what has never been a part of our reality. We tend to push against, we fight, we unintentionally operate in fear due to having a false sense of losing control, which exacerbates the uncertainty of evolving outside the box we've placed ourselves in. That is until we finally feel safe, understood, and get it and give in! By being open, and knowledgeable of how powerful my thoughts and words are. My agenda to consistently press limits, and to not internalize what may go on around me is how I overcame some of the challenges within my role in sports. This is how I continue to handle navigating through various challenges I may encounter, presently.

Yet, having a full understanding that no one is exempt from life's challenges happening to them. I too, over the years have had to become more intentional about prioritizing myself and my well-being. As it is imperative for me to practice what I encourage others to implement. Working in the world of sports is quite demanding with hours in a day that often feels as though they are not enough to do what needs to be done. It became all the more essential that I set aside time to decompress and enjoy the fruits of my labor outside of work. In order for me to have the appropriate personal and work life balance. I implement realistic boundaries, open and effective communication and engage in self-care. This in turn is how I stay motivated and continue to grow as a leader in the ever-evolving world of sports.

Work-life balance is a constant area of improvement for many. However, being aware of that is what makes all the difference in the world. I often find myself in conversations with people from all walks of life where the topic of knowing vs. doing is the difference in most matters. We commonly have thoughts of knowing what adjustments need to be made. Yet, when it comes to doing the work necessary to actually make those changes, we tend to drop the ball and the action(s) required subsequently returns to wishful thinking.

This is why the most important qualities I believe a successful leader in sports should aim to exhibit are self-awareness, emotional intelligence, emotional regulation, humility, integrity, adaptability, the ability to listen to comprehend, the ability to lead and follow by example, to operate with a positive and growth mindset and is authentic.

As I strive daily to display the qualities I identified as most important in efforts to be a successful leader in sports. This too is how I attempt to empower and support other women and girls who aspire to hold leadership positions in sports. We cannot be duplicated and the only person that we can lose to, is ourselves. Once we figure out that we can either be our worst enemy or our biggest cheerleader. It is then we define who we are and how we impact, lead, and grow others.

Furthermore, I would be remiss if I did not address the importance of remembering that we all have a story to tell, while the roads we individually travel may lead to various outcomes. To ensure that we are all able to have positive life changing experiences extended, to further permit our ability to comfortably enjoy the benefits and luxuries obtained from the sacrifices made while working towards our goals.

It is imperative that regardless of our differences of beliefs, race, ethnic backgrounds, sexual orientation/identity, and or socioeconomic statuses, etc. Diversity and inclusion within any space one may be present in. It is paramount to ensure that people feel represented in any environment. It's simple, while you matter, please know that representation matters too!

This is how I have been fortunate to have a number of individuals that have positively influenced me in many ways throughout my career. Specifically, Dr. Javuane Adams-Gaston (Dr. J), who is the Seventh President of Norfolk State University and an American psychologist. As my mentor she has provided the guidance and support needed to make significant strides within my career since transitioning into the world of sports several years ago. As a clinician, operating within an environment that is gradually becoming more inclusive and understanding of the importance of one's mental health and well-being. Dr. J's wisdom and experience as a trailblazer within the sports industry holds a plethora of knowledge. That continues to usher my ability to excel and evolve into a better version of myself personally and professionally.

Overall, we as women are change makers, and that is not up for debate. We are deserving of so much more, which is why I take pride in being a part of this transformation. As a member of the Women Leaders in Sports organization it thoroughly aligns with my professional endeavor that as women to build confidence and leadership you must "Lift as Your Rise!"

So, regardless of the profession a young lady may want to aspire to be within the world of sports. I would simply encourage her to prioritize her mental health, first; find a mentor; to extend herself grace by understanding that she is exactly where she is supposed to be, because if she wasn't she wouldn't be there; I would encourage her to do what's hard and not what's easy, there is no such thing as a shortcut; I would encourage her to give herself PERMISSION to feel the various emotions she may feel, allow them to move through her as she manages them and moves forward; I would encourage her to ask for help when she needs it, as we are not meant to do things alone; I would implore her to mind her own business and redirect the energy she may exert into the people and things she cannot control back into herself; I would encourage her to stay focused, and try not be distracted by what's going on around her; I would remind her that time is not on her side, so, do it NOW; even in the enduring season, when it feels that she is at her weakest point. I would want her to know that this is when she is at her strongest point and surviving what she may feel is breaking her! I would empower her to speak words of encouragement over herself and for her to never forget she is and will always be ENOUGH, and I'm rooting for her!

About Brandy Gresham

Brandy Gresham, a Connecticut native and owner of Morning's Light, LLC devotion and desire to help others, coupled with the love for sports began at a very early age.

Gresham, a graduate of Norfolk State University received her BA in Psychology, and MA in Community and Clinical Psychology. She is a Licensed Professional Counselor, Certified Substance Abuse Counselor, Certified Advance Alcohol and Drug Counselor, and Certified Traumatologist. Gresham is also a Certified Seeking Safety Facilitator and a Mental Health First Aid Trainer.

With 19+ years of collective experience in the Mental Health/Substance Abuse Counseling field and Sports industry. She prides herself in being a woman of integrity and humility, while living her life unapologetically and intentionally. During her leisure she finds solace in spending time with her family and friends, engaging in self-care activities, and remaining spiritually grounded. She is a proud member of Delta Sigma Theta Sorority, Inc.

Monique A. J. Smith

WOMEN WHO LEAD IN SPORTS

Contributing Author: Monique A. J. Smith

A Decade of Saying Yes: From Associate Commissioner to Full Time Entrepreneur

by Monique A. J. Smith

I get to work with individuals either to "Plant Seeds of Empowerment to Lead them to Greatness" or "Guide others to Reach their Desired Destination" in Sports Management Careers. How did I become qualified to be a Guider?

I began my full-time Athletic Administration journey as an "Only" 30-plus years ago, the first full-time woman Sports Information Director within the Central Intercollegiate Athletic Association (CIAA) in 1990, the first woman to receive CIAA Sports Information Director of the Year, and named Interim Athletic Director at Saint Paul's College at 28 years old. Then, I moved up to Division I as the Director of Compliance at the University of Maryland Eastern Shore, after two years the Commissioner of CIAA invited me to the Central Intercollegiate Athletic Association (CIAA). All the while, I was serving on several national committees. And to be honest, I only sometimes handled the pressure of being in a male-dominated industry well. I wrote about the pressure and the beginning of my Athletic Administration journey in the anthology at www.publicfiguremask.com. I wanted to demonstrate to the high achiever woman she needed to protect her mental health to be an effective leader. Managing people can be draining and triggering and can take one off their path of being her/his best self. The most important part I wanted to share was after I began therapy, my career soared within the (CIAA) from being Director of Public Relations to Director Championship to ultimately the number two person as the Senior Woman Administrator and the Director of Governance.

However, after 13 years with the CIAA, I received my "PinkSlip" with the leadership change. Yes, I was disappointed, but the interesting fact is that when I cleaned out my corporate office for over a decade, each item fit perfectly inside my home. It was a sign that to me, I was not going back to a traditional office. Hence, the "PinkSlip" became my "PinkBow," a gift of my full-time entrepreneurship. It has been a decade of being a full-time Leadership Strategist for Athletic Departments/Sport Organizations and individuals who wish to advance in Athletic Administration, Sports Management Careers, or the marketplace.

During this time, I invested in learning how to transform from an educator to an entrepreneur. My consultancy, Seeds of Empowerment®, began in 2005 when I facilitated a retreat for Senior Women Administrators Division III Athletic Conference at the request of a colleague who couldn't make it. The location was only 30 minutes away from me. The conference organizer said, "We were going to pay the scheduled consultant this rate. Does that work for you?" Not expecting any compensation, I was delighted and said yes. I received great feedback and continued to travel to different conferences to deliver leadership messages for Women in Athletics, at the same time doubling up on my reading on leadership trends and creating interactive ways to convey the message.

Even before I began officially consulting, I have always received calls from women in the industry who see blockages to their advancement. Creating an activity is the best way to show how to shift one's thoughts to the other side to see a new perspective and gain the energy to get them through. For example, our "The Walk in Her Shoes" activity highlights this point. It came from my experience of being an Athletic Administrator and having a business office person say, "You just can't come flying in demanding your travel checks because your game is tomorrow. You must first speak and then acknowledge or be aware of what is on our plate before you put anything else on it." The activity incorporates these considerations of other departments at the University to become partners with these questions:

1. Who are their constituents?

2. When is their high-volume season?

3. How can you assist them to assist you?

For example, the University President/Chancellor 'Walk in her Shoes" questions: Who does she answer to? Board, what is the mood and consistency of that board? I learned early in my career that Presidents wake up every day counting their votes. That is a great deal of pressure. Strategic decisions are made and often appear as retreats or punting but are preparatory to come back and fight another day.

Hence, in 2013, I was free to do these workshops full-time. I was blessed to be on retainer with the NCAA Leadership Development office to go across the country delivering leadership workshops for student-athletes and athletic staff and coaches. Around that time, I had a publicist who asked if I wanted to be the host or the guest on a podcast. I said I had control issues; I would be the host. I joined the Survival Radio Network with the show "Chat in the Garden with Monique" in August 2013. I selected the language of a garden to represent a place to grow. The most impactful Yes was yes to the requirement to create a private Facebook group to engage with the podcast's audience. One decade later, the "Garden" has bloomed into 3,000 members.

Around 2015, the NCAA national office changed leadership as well. The focus went from education to enforcement, and the NCAA no longer needed my services. I could continue to deliver university workshops, but now payment came to me directly instead of through the NCAA.

As that door closed, a window of opportunity appeared. I was conducting my last staff retreat on behalf of the NCAA at Cheyney University when an Old Dominion University (ODU) Professor called on my phone. She said she had attended my Black Women in Sport Foundation Forum that I curated and moderated, and she needed an Adjunct in a week. I said yes, but a year later, I received a call from the Hampton University Chairperson of Sports Management asking if I could teach Sports Management courses. I said yes, again. That began my six years as an Adjunct.

The same year of the NCAA transition, I began to host LeadYourShip Retreats at my business-owned timeshares. The transformational results have been excellent. Some alumni are now Director of Athletics on the University and Interscholastic Level, and one attendee is a High-level Girl Scout Executive representing two States. One is the head coach at the Junior College Level, two advanced from high school to college level administration, several received their doctorates, and one is an international speaker/consultant on Diversity, Equity, and Inclusion (DEI).

Although this was very successful, coordinating dates became problematic, which is when ZOOM hit the screen. We evolved to an online subscription membership that provides access to training and networking, a group coaching program called Advance Academy. We meet every month for a mastermind; the recordings go into a vault for self-paced learning. Each member has an individualized learning plan, receives a leadership ebook every quarter, and initially attends a one-on-one strategy session with me that includes completing assessments. Here are some of the transformation's alums: One was a stay-at-home mom to Athletic Administrator to now a sitting VP/Director of Athletics, another one has hosted the Black Student-Athlete Summit on campus,

another created the NFL experienceships with Historically Black Colleges and Universities (HBCU) students. The program provides tools for confidence, the network offers community, and I give place to communicate feelings.

The latest product created to guide others to their next has been the "Significance in Athletics and Sports ™ Magazine. Previously, I had launched the Speaker's Bureau to assist women in the "Garden" who asked how to get speaking engagements, how to get consulting opportunities, and how to advance. I kept saying we have to let people know you are an expert. We have to indulge in "Expert Marketing" and package your specialized knowledge in a format people can digest and want to continue to hear and work with you. So, I said, invest in "Expert Marketing" training with me, and we will create your launching pad to reach your desired destination, but you must plant the seed in places you want to Bloom. Today, we have six issues on Amazon, and the seventh one is in production and will go live on Amazon in the Spring of 2024. We are accepting for Fall 2024.

I am blessed to share my knowledge, lead others out of bitterness to betterment, and guide them to their desired destination. All glory to God, for he says, "Being confident of this very thing, that he which hath begun a good work in me will perform it until the day of Jesus Christ." Philippians 1:6 Because of that, I said "Yes."

About Monique A. J. Smith

Monique A.J. Smith, is a Leadership Strategist that guides Athletics Departments/Sport Organizations and Individuals who wish to advance in Athletics Administration/Sports Management careers through her company, Seeds of Empowerment® LLC. Smith, a Sports Management veteran of 30 plus years, was Adjunct Faculty at Hampton University teaching Sports Management Courses. Fall 2023, Monique published her 6th issue of Significance in Athletics and Sports, that features Black Women sharing their 'Specialized Knowledge' in the Industry. All issues can be found at www.seedsofempowermentstore.com or Amazon. She is most known for her 10 seasons as the host of the internationally recognized weekly podcast "A Chat in the Garden with Monique A.J. Smith", that spotlights Women of Color in Athletics/Sports to her 3K Followers.

Smith's time in Collegiate Athletics includes a 13 year tenure as athletic conference executive for the historic Central Intercollegiate Athletic Association (CIAA). She also served in various athletic administrative roles on the campuses of Saint Paul's College and the University of Maryland Eastern Shore within a ten year period. Smith was a member of the Adjunct Faculty at Old Dominion University in Norfolk, Virginia.

With the understanding that knowledge is the key to success, Smith customizes her presentations to provide clients with leadership tools to prepare them to make informed decisions. Monique has dedicated her life to marketing the success of others, developing opportunities for the underrepresented and influencing decision makers to embrace diversity and inclusion. These actions have led to extraordinary opportunities to facilitate change and see strives in the development of others.

Dr. Jillian McNiff Villemaire

WOMEN WHO LEAD IN SPORTS

Contributing Author: Dr. Jillian McNiff Villemaire

A Journey of Resilience, Reinvention, and Sports Leadership

by Dr. Jillian McNiff Villemair

My journey through the intricate web of sports, education, and personal growth began in a small Massachusetts town. The eldest of four siblings, I was introduced to the world of sports at a young age, navigating my way through dance classes, cheerleading, and softball. Although not a standout athlete, my competitive spirit and unwavering dedication paved the way for my leadership role as the captain of high school cross country and track and field teams.

After high school, I attended Westfield State College (now Westfield State University) as a Movement Science, Sport and Leisure Studies major focused on Athletic Training while a cross country athlete. An untimely injury interrupted my competitive running career, prompting a reevaluation of my career trajectory. Unyielding in her determination, I recognized the limited opportunities for women in the male-dominated realm of athletic training. Opting for a strategic pivot, I delved into business-focused classes, eventually steering my academic journey towards sport management.

Despite the absence of a dedicated sport management major at Westfield State, I seized the opportunity to broaden my skills through additional courses and internships. These experiences included stints with the athletic department, an event planning position, a minor league hockey team, and the prestigious Basketball Hall of Fame. As graduation approached, I cast my net wide, applying to both jobs and graduate schools, ultimately securing a last-minute graduate assistantship at the University of Nevada Las Vegas.

In the bustling landscape of Las Vegas, I immersed myself in the study of Sport and Leisure Service Management. I wore multiple hats, serving as a teaching and research assistant while delving into internships with various sports entities, including the Las Vegas 51s, Chicago Bears, Boston Celtics, and the New England Patriots and Revolution. My journey eventually led me to a full-time role with the New England Patriots and Revolution, where I spent four seasons as the Client Services Coordinator in the marketing department. I managed client partnerships and sponsorship fulfillment as part of this role.

Simultaneously, I discovered a newfound passion for teaching during my time as an adjunct instructor at Lasell College. The energy drawn from students fueled my commitment to education, prompting me to teach night classes while employed by the Kraft Sports Group. This dual role continued until I transitioned to Boston University's Fitness and Recreation Center. Here, I embarked on a journey to earn a doctorate in education, encapsulating my dedication to both academia and the sports industry.

The year 2011 marked a significant juncture as I accepted a full-time teaching position at Mount Ida College. My role as a sport management instructor and Faculty Athletics Representative provided a fulfilling blend of academia and hands-on engagement with athletes. This intersection became my" sweet spot," embodying the perfect equilibrium she sought in her professional life.

In 2013, armed with a completed dissertation on the early career experiences of sport management graduates, I graduated from Boston University. Subsequently, I relocated to St. Augustine, Florida, where I currently impart my wealth of knowledge at Flagler

College. Passionate about nurturing the next generation of sports professionals, I developed a faculty athletics mentorship program, adding an extra layer of support for student-athletes.

A perpetual learner, my commitment to education extends beyond the conventional. Certifications as a DISC Consultant and Athlete Development Specialist underscore her dedication to understanding the nuances of human behavior in the sports landscape. As I balance professional pursuits, I find solace in family time, chasing after her three active children, and reveling in the joy of sports. The pages of my journey continue to unfold, each chapter a testament to resilience, adaptability, and an enduring love for the world where sports and education intersect.

Considerations:

Were there any challenges or barriers that existed? If so, what were they and how did you navigate them?

Did you have any mentors along the way?

What can you share with young women athletes just beginning their sports journey?

About Dr. Jillian McNiff Villemaire

Dr. Jillian McNiff Villemaire holds the title of Associate Professor and Program Director of Sport Management at Flagler College in the picturesque city of St. Augustine, Florida. A true New Englander at heart, she was born and raised in Massachusetts, where her passion for sports ignited during her formative years, shaping her into a lifelong Boston sports enthusiast.

Having delved into the dynamic realm of the sports industry, Dr. Villemaire discovered a profound calling in education. Transitioning from a sports industry practitioner to an esteemed educator, she found fulfillment in guiding and shaping the aspirations of future leaders preparing for impactful careers.

Beyond the confines of academia, Dr. Villemaire immerses herself in the boundless joys of family life, where her three remarkably active children keep her days filled with laughter and shared adventures. Her journey, a captivating blend of sports, academia, and family, unfolds as a testament to her commitment to both the professional development of her students and the cherished moments with her loved ones.

Women Who Lead In Sports

Kathleen Dorinda Williams

WOMEN WHO LEAD IN SPORTS
Contributing Author: Kathleen Dorinda Williams

The Power of Perseverance

by Kathleen Dorinda Williams

Perseverance as defined by Merriam-Webster, is the "continued effort to do or achieve something despite difficulties, failure, or opposition" and the Oxford Languages program defines it as, "persistence in doing something despite difficulty or delay in achieving success". I do not always get it right, but I will work to always be the version of myself, and I invite you to do the same. You ever find yourself thinking back over a time or situation, in life and say to yourself, how did I get here? Where did it all begin? Throughout this chapter, you will see leadership attributes or qualities bolded and, in a moment, it may have surfaced with meaning in my life. I urge you to think upon them, maybe write them down and in your quiet time, think about what they mean in the context of your journey, now or in the future. they are not all inclusive for you or I.

Life, Sports and Leadership - I had to think back on what inspired me to pursue sports and how that pursuit contributed to the development of the leader I am today. You may not see me as the traditional sports leader you expected to read about but my hope is there is something here that you may identify with or be able to utilize in your journey. My connection to sports began when I met a coach who saw potential in me and my experiences with sports from that moment forward transformed my life, forever. My leadership in sports became more about how my then, shaped my future self, on this marathon called Life. It helped to reinforce and embed my never give up attitude, the importance of teamwork, spirit to succeed with integrity and no matter how hard it may get, sometimes you have to encourage not only yourself but others amid dire circumstances. I learned to take the lead, be solution-focused, and adaptable! If a task is given to me to get it done, I will give my all to accomplish whatever it is, like making sure the baton crosses the finish line. A few years ago, one of my colleagues gave me a mug and it literally said, "Get It Done". I took a deep breath and smiled, because it captured a core attribute of who I am but I am clear, but I did not become who I am by myself.

Stepping back, there I was, this long-legged girl whose family moved a lot and was trying to find my space and place. I was looking for that place to contribute, I was looking for acceptance, connection and belonging among my peers. You see, I was the shy girl, whose light was flickering, and sometimes simply dim due to life's circumstances, none of which I recall picking, but they seemed to pick me. I was trying to protect myself as I had experienced some traumatic situations and staying to myself was safe or around people I perceived as safe. Looking back, I saw myself as a late bloomer, who on top of everything else, I had to continuously make friends due to the moves, until high school. People around me would comment on my long legs and automatically assume I should play basketball. My mother, a hard worker, kept my sister and I active, balanced with working two jobs most of our formative years. The depth of her work ethic was a life-long example for me. She put me in recreational basketball and let us just say, while I was very coordinated, mainly on the dance floor, it disappeared each time I had a ball in my hand. I was still growing into those legs. The other sport continuously referenced was track and field. "I bet you can run fast with those long legs".

But it was not until high school, when an opportunity presented itself, it seemed like we were laying down roots and I knew I would graduate from this high school. I had a coach, who also was a teacher, approach, and ask me to consider running cross-country. I shared that I am going to run track and he thought it would help build my endurance for track in the spring – they were trying to build a team and not many, if any, girls were running cross-country at my high school. I gave it a try and the rest was history. I ran year-round, cross-country, then indoor track and outdoor track – I was a middle– and long-distance runner. I placed and medaled, met and beat personal records, and went to the Penn Relays, individually and as a team. It was humbling, exciting and I found my voice on the field. Yes, it felt good to see that my hard work mattered, it filled my cup. I, the team, made a difference, positive contributions within the team and the school. A larger by-product of this season was lifting fellow teammates with passion and energy. **(Relationship building)** My senior year of high school, I was the captain of our cross-country team and became the first female in my high school's history to qualify and run in the State of Maryland Cross-Country competition. I was honored as female athlete of the year – all very humbling experiences. I was uniquely me and more comfortable in my own skin. I was not the fastest, but I was steady and took my commitment seriously and excelled. I was constantly learning my craft - adjusting, strategizing, adapting to climate, fine tuning my stride, baton pass and more. **(Learn, Practice and Application)** Be very clear, it was not all a bed of roses, my academics were on point, but socially as the new transplant student, I experienced some bullying and demoralizing moments, yet I endured. God would send a few loyal friends into my space, there was another runner who is my earliest best girlfriend. Our friendship connected two high schools, inspiring the teams to root for and support each other. **(Inspiration -**

Commordary - Influence) I was a determined student and athlete.

I continued my sports journey through my junior year of college at the University of Richmond, a predominately white institution (PWI). Being a student athlete in college was not an easy feat for this first generation African American female college student, in uncharted waters, as one of about nine other female students like myself. How could I expect it to be? The pressure, the unknown and scars of the past and then feeling "alone" initially, on a college campus with a lot of people who did not look like me and many with limited exposure. **(Growth and Courage).** While it was an institution committed to diversity, it would take time and not everyone was not committed. I believed if I could make it there, I could make it anywhere. I was raised to remember, we all "put our pants on one leg at a time" and no one is better than anyone else. In college, I had to be open to an extent and understood that I would do almost as much teaching as I did learn. How did I learn to give and support others? Genuinely smile in the face of obstacles - knowing whose I am, not who I am. **(Vulnerability and Humility)** I am grateful for the angels on campus, prayer warriors at home, and other contributors along my path. Not all of the contributors had my best interest at heart, but I grew in the process. Showing up and giving it my all running is what I knew so I walked on the track there and by the end of my freshman year, I was one of a few freshmen left. Also, that first semester was the worst and hardest of my life, from sickness to academic challenges but I did not give up. I was carrying more than myself, and failure was not an option. Early on I learned to take my moment and then sit up, brush myself off, refocus and move forward. Oh, not always easy but necessary, then and now. When you think something cannot be done, sometimes we just need to take that moment, and re-imagine. Then, I may not have said it was God directly but today, for me, I am clear, when God places something on my heart, in my spirit, I pursue it despite the naysayers, set-backs, nervousness or delays. **(Determination)**

Through it all, I know that on this wider stage of life, hard work, dedication, belief in something better or greater existed not just for me but other young women who can relate to me. Is that you or someone you know? I matter, you matter, we all matter. Sports inspires and empowers young women. I have seen this in my own daughter, a trailblazer in her own right. She played soccer from elementary through high school. Her senior year, there were not enough students to form a Varsity girls' team, so she integrated the Varsity boys team - it became a co-ed Varsity Team. It only takes one to make a change. **(Modeling)**

The things that we go through are not to kill us but to illuminate paths, plant seeds, prepare, and initiate a pruning process in our lives. Throughout my life, no matter how dire the situation, how devastated I may have felt, there was the feeling that I could not give up. **(Persistence)** I did not get here on my own, no one does. And like many of you, I evolve continually, we all have the opportunity to evolve into our better and best self. In times when I may have not felt seen nor heard, there was somebody, a mom, dad, teacher, a coach, bus driver, auntie, big Mama, Nana - someone praying or believing for our success, creating opportunities, sacrificing behind the scene. For me, ultimately, I know God was there. It is not always easy, and may take several iterations over time, of processing and reflection. Our painful and difficult situations can turn into positive fuel for our rebounds, passion and purpose. And there is a blessing in the press and everything happens for a reason, even when we do not understand it at the time. Do not ignore what is going on with you but if you have experienced being counted out; made to feel less than, talk about, instead of to you; keep pressing. My mom would sometimes say, they talked about Jesus, what makes you special – at the time, I did not understand the depth of the response but later I did.

I believe that God has put gifts and talents inside of each of us and the adults in our lives, when we are young, are responsible to help cultivate our gifts and expose us to different opportunities so that you can see the world is bigger than you could ever imagine. And in our adult life, leaders serve or inspire to do this similarly. I know God has put something inside of you and I that no one else has and that the development of those gifts and talents will change the world in a way that no one else can. This is for everyone, so take a moment to think and write down those things that you uniquely bring, pull at your mind and heart in the quiet moments. If nothing comes, that only means it may be deeper or vaster than you realize, possibly hidden under the vicissitudes of life. Talk with someone you trust, and/or unbiased trusted third party. There are always areas to continue to develop and fine tune as a leader. There are various stages of leadership development, sometimes impacted by your position or simply stage in life. **(Mentor and Coach)**

I believe my life experiences, circumstances, and upbringing strongly shaped my foundation as a leader and there are areas that I am still developing. As I reflect on the age-old debate as to whether leaders are born or made, I believe it is a combination of both observing leaders around me and reflecting on my own leadership development. As an oldest child, for example, I took on leading certain aspects at home as my mother's helper; I learned how to process information quickly, focus on outcomes, completing tasks, timelines, and order. **(Solution-focused)** I bring these attributes into my professional spaces today, to various degrees. And simultaneously, over the years, I continue to learn or refine new skills from better delegation, increasing my emotional intelligence in lower areas to develop team members beyond their current position. Leadership is a privilege not a right. Leaders never stop developing, learning, fine tuning existing skills and challenging oneself to new areas and ways of thinking. Everyone can be a leader. Leadership is not about the title someone has, it is about learning, application, and authentic implementation of leadership characteristics. Development as a leader has brought some discomfort and it should. As Proverbs 27:17 tells us, "As iron sharpens iron, so one person sharpens another." We should gleam from each other. **(Empowerment)** Think about it, has your greatest professional growth or life lessons come about due to smooth or challenging situations? I have experienced this in leadership roles, past and present. Leadership is intrinsically first leading yourself, then about the opportunity to positively contribute to another person's growth and aptitude. Serving in leadership roles allows us to learn and believe and support someone, seeing what they may not see in themselves or build up areas they aspire to develop or improve and create a safe space to expand their professional wings. Perhaps pave the way to give someone a chance that someone gave or did not give you, or that you passed up with regret later. Sometimes you will see yourself in another person. That is not for you to treat them like they are you, but it may provide an empathic lens or connection to reach them in ways someone else may not be able. It is important to be aware of implicit bias as well. I believe that God expects us to open doors for others – a hand up, not hand-out. Our success is bigger than us. There is someone out there waiting for you – Their destiny is tied to your dreams, gifts, and talents. Making a difference in this world may depend on you stepping up.

It is important to understand that everyone will not be happy about your commitment, grind, level of integrity or gifts. For women of color in leadership, it is often with challenges that others experience much less, if at all. Microaggressions and stereotypes are real. A few of the challenges or observations from my own experience or that of other women of color endure include, not being taken as seriously as a male or white female counterpart and being characterized by the stereotypes that make other people comfortable in the world of business. For example, if a leader is upset, maybe even angry about a situation, instead of attributing it to an inciting, unfair or frustrating situation it is attributed to her personality as opposed to her outrage about the situation. Those are two different things, it is not an internal characteristic, it is due to an external stimulus. I am a very passionate and feeling person, especially when it comes to what I care about and that transcends into all of the work I have done or contributed to, in communities, over the years, whether supporting pregnant or parenting teens, misunderstood pubescent boys, underserved and traumatized individuals. And I would be remiss to not acknowledge that we must be cognizant of our communication styles. We have to make sure we are hard on the problem and not the people. We must take accountability. At times, I have seen this create a disconnect between my own intention and how information was received. And another aspect to consider is if you are someone who also subscribes to being passive or passive-aggressive because of feeling uncomfortable in a situation or other things within oneself left unaddressed. We have to ask ourselves who shows up and if we know this is an area that needs attention, put in the work and you will be better for it in the long run as it will improve the relationships and collaborations around you. **(Communication)** We, as women, especially with the myths regarding women of color, should support, lift, mentor each other and, familiarity does not give us a pass to be messy, do the bare minimum, pull each other down but instead put our best foot forward. If anything, we should want to step up our game even more for each other, people who look like us or could be us. Yes, being a leader can be tough, lonely, and thankless in moments and it can also be rewarding, invigorating and inspiring. In leadership, self-care is an essential element, and it is a balancing act and no one gets it right all the time. An important note, sometimes an attribute that has served you well in one space will not in another level of leadership or situation and you may have to change your approach. Be open to that. Rest and know that your gift will make room for you. In my life God has kept me. Learn to let your faith be bigger than your fear. As leaders, we must understand that we are accountable for the energy we bring into a space – What energy will you bring into the next space?

Five years ago, I was told that I had an autoimmune disease, out of nowhere. I was in and out of the hospital over the next 18 months, with no warning, scheduled procedures and I continued to work, full-time. Doctors explained there was no cure. The only long-term option was a whole organ, liver transplant. After going through the rigorous process to be approved for the transplant list, I received a call three and a half weeks later I was blessed with a liver match – two surgeries and extensive recovery (six months later) – At any point, due to the pain, pressure and unknown, I could have given up but I persevered — Every aspect of who I am has been tested and I am gratefully still here. The leader I am and evolving into is foundationally based on what I learned through my personal sports journey and life. Know that opportunities knock, and miracles do happen. Step into your destiny, someone is counting on it. If there was one word that would equal the sum total of my life, it would be perseverance and not always of my own fruition but because of the God that loves and keeps me. **(Faith)**

About Kathleen Dorinda Williams

K. Dorinda Williams, Owner and Founder of *KD Integrity Signing Services* and *Heart for Community Consulting*. Working in community is generationally weaved, coupled with her education and experience has allowed her the honor of empowering, educating and supporting communities for over 25 years. For the last 12 years, Dorinda has worked for a Washington, DC Non-profit that dually connects to her core beliefs.

She is solution focused and is known as someone who "Gets It Done". Dorinda believes that it is essential to provide meaningful support, services, and opportunities to assist individuals reach their full potential – happy, healthy, and whole.

She holds a master's degree in Public Health from George Washington University and Bachelor of Arts in Biology from the University of Richmond. She is a Certified Health Education Specialist and recently, Dorinda became a Maryland Commissioned Notary and licensed MD TIPIC/Notary Signing Agent.

Dorinda perseveres, is dedicated and determined.

Women Who Lead In Sports

Nicole Henry

WOMEN WHO LEAD IN SPORTS
Sports World | Nicole Trotter Henry

Sports World

by Nicole Trotter Henry

Before I can tell you my story, I have to start with **HIS**tory. The history of my love for sports and how I got to where I am today is because of four men in my life. The man who made me, my father, Claude R. Trotter Jr., my father-in-law, Charles W. Henry, my childhood best friend's father, Major Boyd and last but not least my sweet husband Keith D. Henry.

Claude Russell Trotter Jr., was a big kid, 6"4 with good bones, my father grew up in Raleigh, North Carolina playing sports. He was a three-sport athlete at Ligon High School, baseball, football and basketball. After high school, dad went on to play college football on scholarship at Hampton Institute (now Hampton University). He played Defensive End, and Special Teams field goal kicker and punt return. This is where he met my mother, Ordee (Delores) Eaton, they married and had two children, my brother Claude the III and myself, then Nicole Ordee Trotter.

Charles William Henry, my father-in-law, was a 6"2, 4-sport athlete from Newton, North Carolina, where he graduated from Central High School. While at Central dad ran 4.35 in track, earning the nickname rabbit, All Conference in basketball, football and baseball. This earned Charles an athletic scholarship to attend Shaw University in Raleigh, North Carolina. Charles's father died tragically during this time, so leaving the obligation to help his mom fell on him and his sister. Because of this dad stayed home and worked at the local mill providing for his family for many years to come. At the age of 25 dad took up refereeing softball, then baseball and basketball. This passion for refereeing took him all over the east coast for over 52 years of "calling ball".

Because of segregation or the lack of integration, both men were not known as today's five-star recruits, they didn't get to take advantage of "Name Image and Likeness' ' either, but for me they are the real five-star athletes in the family.

Dr. Major Michanelangelo Boyd, was a native of Rocky Mount North Carolina but I knew him best when he lived in Raleigh. He had two daughters, Michelle and Marcelle, often adding me to the dinner table. I called him dad too, and loved to watch him referee college basketball and football when we could go. Daddy Boyd was an African American handsome man and had an infectious smile. He started his basketball refereeing career in 1961 and ended it in the mid 90s. His career took him to become a Division 1 referee for the CIAA, MEAC and ACC for basketball and football. In the early 1970s Boyd served as President of the North Carolina Athletic Officials Association. In 1988, he was named "CIAA basketball referee of the year." Before his career ended, he was a two- time Hall of Fame inductee into the CIAA and MEAC. Even though he retired from the sport, encouraging people to go into refereeing did not stop. He inspired me, because he was professional, sharp in his calls (mechanics), and oftentimes he was the only in the referee crew that looked like me. This is where HIStory starts, and I have always looked up to all four of these wonderful men for that.

Early Years

At the age of 10 years old, I went to live with my father in Raleigh, NC. My mother and father had divorced and even though my mother loved my brother and I very much, she struggled with the demands of motherhood, now that she was single. The last day of my fifth-grade year, a Wednesday. I couldn't take it anymore. The fights with my brother and the loneliness of being home, A LOT, made me want to go live with my dad. I picked up the phone and said, "Dad I can't take it anymore, come get me" and that Wednesday evening after work, he drove to Hampton, Virginia and returned to Raleigh, with me. His days of raising a little girl and being what we know today as a "girl dad" began. I wasn't a prissy girl, I was just the opposite, a Tom boy. So much so dad made me vow to wear one dress or skirt a week to show my feminine side. I loved sports, outside with the boys we were very competitive, and no one was a match. Dad and I would watch ACC basketball or football games and would have to threaten me to go to bed as I looked over his shoulders during the national basketball championships.

Girls back in the day didn't start playing basketball as young as they do now. We didn't have YMCA girls' leagues, but I did have a park, Roberts Park, right up the street. It wasn't popular for girls to play with the boys, so I watched mostly even though I soon became a lot taller than most of the boys. By my seventh-grade year, basketball tryouts came around. Dad said for me to go to tryouts, so I did. I will never forget hearing the coach say, "alright, line up and do layups" …." hmmm what's a layup?" I thought. I didn't know what a lay-up was, I didn't know what a free throw was, I'd seen it on TV but never tried it myself. I was a terrible basketball player. Dad said, because I was so tall, almost 6 feet at 13 years old, I would make the basketball team, and I did. The first year I didn't see much court time, but I was determined to work hard and do better by the eighth-grade season. Eighth grade season came, I was so much improved, I was awarded Carroll Middle School's girls basketball MVP.

In high school I struggled with basketball, I could have gone to my assigned school, Sanderson, but it was too far away. There I would have had plenty of playing time, but because dad was working a lot out of town, and my grandparents had to come across town to get me, I had to settle for a closer alternative, Enloe High. Enloe was a good school but I played behind several girls that went on to play basketball in college. Enloe had a great girls' team, we were always on top of the conference charts, but my playing time was not there. My heart was hurt, and my self-esteem was low, I was taller by this time, 6 '1 but I couldn't improve by sitting on the bench. Because of this I had no aspirations to play in college.

College

After high school graduation, I went on to North Carolina A&T State University. These were the best years of my life. My love for sports blossomed even more. Our football team was often #1 in the conference and the "Ws" were infectious, so I wanted more. I was offered an opportunity to work up in the college football office. Today, the girls and guys have fancy titles and are called "recruiting assistants or recruiting coordinators". Some of these positions today could have an hourly wage with them as well. I worked in the football office many hours and my pay was using a rotary telephone to call home to mom, dad and our grandma, I worked for free long distance.

For many seasons I was one of a few consistent office student workers the football program had. The coaches were like my surrogate fathers for me. If my car broke down, or advice was needed Coaches like Joe Godette, Kenny Phillips, Mark Saunders or John Eder were there to help out. Well, my senior came, and Coach Godette said to me, "Hey Nik there's a Graduate Assistant coach coming in, great guy, we want you to meet him." I wasn't crazy about the idea, mixing work with pleasure wasn't my cup of tea so I brushed the idea under the rug. A few days later, I saw this fine, nice athletic body of a young man walk down the hall with his ball cap tipped downward and God spoke to me and said, "that is your husband". I couldn't believe it, Pastor Joel Osteen, calls it "a still small voice," and yes, that is what I heard.

Women Who Lead In Sports

Keith D. Henry was his name, a graduate assistant coach, or GA from Maiden, North Carolina. Keith had graduated from Catawba College, in Salisbury, North Carolina, a Division 2 (D2) school. He played football, free safety, and from what I hear to this very day he was a VERY good player. He must have been a good athlete because he went on to be inducted into Catawba College Hall of Fame and the SAC 8 Conference Hall of Fame. The stories that people often tell is when he hit a guy so hard on the field, the player had to be carried off on a stretcher, he was a beast.

Keith came into the football office one day, I was on the phone talking to Mama Flucker, my grandmother in Cleveland; remember free long distance. Grandma was talking about BINGO, church bake sales, etc. Keith walks in and says, "Um… you that girl I'm supposed to meet?" I nodded in disbelief of the NERVE, does he not see me on the phone, RUDE. He goes on to say, "well ummm …. how bout you come down to the fieldhouse after practice and see me" and he turns and walks out the room. "Ooooo" I thought, "who does he think I am," he didn't know I was raised by a man. My father taught me, a young man was to come to me, and most did not approve of women chasing them. I told grandma I would call her back. I looked up the number to the field house and on the rotary phone, I dialed the numbers and called down to the field house. "Coach Godette, I don't know who this young man you want me to meet, but please tell him I live at 121 Curtis Hall, he can find me there" and with an attitude, I hung up the phone. Now, I have told this story 100 times but if Keith is around when I tell it, he is quick to say, "she came down to the field house".

Keith and I dated and fell in love my senior year. He as a GA and me as a student worker, we did initially receive some grief from the administration, for our relationship. We worked through it though and took our relationship slow. These were LEAN times for us, he didn't get paid very much as a GA, housing, classes and a meal ticket was all paid for, so extra funds came with his parents visit, Keith's third shift UPS job, or my monthly allowance from dad. We spent a lot of quality time together and I knew he was the one. Keith and I married in 1995, and soon after returning from the honeymoon, he got a job offer to work in Athens, Ohio at Ohio University. My life as a College coaches' wife began.

Coach's Wife

I started into the wonderful sisterhood of being a college coaches' wife in 1995. I was 25 years old, not long from college myself and a newlywed. Keith, now my husband, took a job in Athens, Ohio. Rev. Jesse Jackson, came and spoke in Athens County and deemed Athens as the poorest county in the state of Ohio, but it was a college town in the MAC conference so most didn't notice. Even though I was born in the northern part of Ohio, Shaker Heights, this southeastern area was very foreign to me. Keith and I didn't have very much. What we did have, we loaded up in a UHAUL truck, fish and tank sloshing back and forth in the front cab, and we were going up the West Virginia mountains to start our new journey in life. On the highway, I saw a lot of mountains, a lot of cows and corn fields. I saw the police perched behind a billboard stationed on the ground, like a scene from the Andy Griffith Show. When we got to Athens, we moved into a little, old apartment complex, United Roofing Apartments. Unfortunately, it too had a huge cow pasture behind us with several stinky cows. I cried! One of the OU assistant football coaches, Troy Calhoun (Head Coach of Air Force today) was kind enough to come help us unload the truck. "T-Roy, " as we called him, didn't know coming to help us could have cost him his life that day. Troy was helping Keith take our huge, extremely heavy, dresser up the steps to the second floor. Keith was at the top of the steps and Troy was pushing it up from the bottom on a dolly. There was a strap supporting the move, but the strap snapped free…UGH!! The dresser came loose, and it became too much for Troy to handle and it bolted down the steps at top speed. I was nearby in the kitchen and I heard screams, and as I ran into the living room, Troy stopped, dropped and rolled on the floor, out the way, to safety. The downstairs apartment door was wide open and the dresser came down the steps with such force, it hit the door and snapped the front door knob clean out of the socket. I knew God was with Troy that day, because even now, every time I see him, I tell him, "we thank God that the dresser didn't kill you."

So now I have left my family. They were seven hours away, Keith's family was five hours away, I had cows in my backyard, I unpacked and set up house in two days, no friends nearby............I cried again. What made it worse, on TV that week, Stuart Scott, ESPN commentator, announced Ohio University, the school Keith is coaching, had the LONGEST losing streak in the nation. I cried. "Where do you have me?" is all I kept thinking, but because of football game losses, the previous staff got fired, wiping out all nine assistants and the head coach. This is why we were hired to come turn the football program around, and our first, of several, rebuilding of a program begins.

Not long after we arrived, our very sweet head coaches' wife Holly Grobe, decided to have a bridal shower for Andrea Mullen, another wife and myself. Andrea and I both had just gotten married so Holly thought this would be a great time for all the OU coaches' wives to get together and meet, she was right. At this event, our sisterhood began and several of us are all still very close today. See, Athens was and still is a very isolated town, a true "College Town." Not much shopping for us there, a grocery store or two, a Roses and a JCPenney's were featured at the strip mall, is about all we had. Athens had even fewer restaurants, a McDonalds, Miller's Chicken (the best fried chicken and macaroni salad ever) and a Bob Evans were some of the only real choices in the area. Our airport, real restaurants, and shopping malls were either 45 minutes to Parkersburg, West Virginia, or an hour and a half to Columbus, Ohio.

Women Who Lead In Sports

Not all football coaching staff are like this, some women, for whatever reason, don't always get along. We range from different ages, walks of life, ethnicities, religions, children, no children but with this staff at OU we genuinely loved each other.

Our first season was rough, remember, the longest losing streak in the nation. This was also hard on me because I was at NC A&T State University where losing was never the norm, so I had to adapt. At OU, the football crowd, if any, always left right after the band was playing at halftime. The band was known to be better than the OU football team. They had their own CD out which was unheard of back then or even now, but they were GOOD! Our first win came a few games into the season and when we won the OU students stormed the field and tore down the goal post………. whhhhat!! you gotta be kidding me. This was the first time I had seen this.

As we improved, our staff changed a bit, coaches got jobs and better opportunities to upgrade their position in the profession. Each year Coach Grobe allowed us a "wives trip." This is one away game a year, the school would pay for the coaches' wives to go to a football game, with no children, just us. This trip was an all-expense paid vacation or a time to have our husbands for a bit, between meetings, and the stress of the game. We usually knew where we were going because every year it would be the trip the furthest away. The best trip of course was when we went to play at the University of Hawaii and the wives were treated to go as well. It always helps when you play a non-conference game, you are considered the underdog and we come in and get wined and dined and we win the game. The plane ride home was always sweeter when that happened.

During the years at Ohio University, and many of Keith's games, I don't think I missed a one until recent years, because the boys started playing their own sports. So, with that I have seen a lot of football, and I love it. As a wife, though, it has been hard to sit in the stands and hear fans talk "shit" about your husband or the "play calling," when people don't understand that it's not always on the coach. It's not always easy depending on 18- or 19-year-old kids, who might be sick, just broke up with his girlfriend or just having a bad day, to get our paycheck every month. I have seen wives almost get into physical fights or verbal altercations because of this, so to help my stress level, I learned to bring a stroller and put one of my smaller kids in it and walk around the stadium during game time. Now, don't get me wrong, I love watching these games, but for years at Ohio University and schools beyond, games were VERY close and VERY stressful. One day I looked at my husband and said, "Now, I know why I married you." He said, "why" with a glazed look on his face, "so I can get into football games for free" we both laughed.

One of my most memorable games was the year 1997 OU played Marshall University in Huntington, West Virginia. It was towards the end of the season and the weather was horrible. This was my first AND LAST game that I would sit in the snow, sleet, rain, then snow, sleet and rain. During part of the game, it had to be stopped for the snowplows to come and blow the snow away so the officials and team could see the lines on the field. We were doing well that season and felt optimistic about this game but there was one kid on the Marshall team that was a problem………"Randy Moss" Randy Moss, we kept hearing about, a great wide receiver, a freak on the football field and he showed us true form that day. After that game was over, and we lost, I vowed that day that if I came back to Marshall, I would be in a restaurant down the street watching the games, and I did. Randy set a NCAA record on us, making his 50th catch breaking a single season touchdown record. He then got a penalty for throwing the touchdown football out of the stadium to the next-door McDonald's parking lot. Years later, I refereed Randy's daughter in a North Carolina basketball tournament and told him I was still mad at him for that "ass whipping" that he alone gave us, on that bitter cold day.

Another game that was very memorable was after we were at Wake Forest University. Used to be when we first joined the ACC conference, people would see Wake Forest on the schedule and would put an immediate "Loss" down for Wake Forest but, we redshirted a lot of freshman, giving them a year to get prepared, and found a number of boys we called "diamonds in the rough" or other schools didn't want. Well, this particular season, we were

winning and we were playing Clemson University down in the backwoods of Clemson, South Carolina. I had the children with me at the game, it was freezing cold. In 2004, Wake and Clemson battled it out so much we went into a double overtime loss. The refs were cheating Wake so badly, calling a fake "pass interference" I said "they aren't going to let us out of here with a win", there is some true "home cooking" going on here. The bitter cold was just as bad as the bitter crowd, I couldn't watch the game and I couldn't stand the cold. We lost, 37-30, I was sooo mad, I said that day, "Oh, this school gets on my nerves, I'm never coming back!"………. .I actually said the worst things that I had to ask for forgiveness. Be careful what you say, you are "never going to do," KJ, our oldest son, spent five wonderful years playing college football for those Clemson Tigers, and we loved every minute of it, "home cooking and all ".

November 2008, Thursday night on ESPN, another Clemson game we played Wake Forest again at Wake and we beat them 12-7. This unforgivable loss caused Clemson's then Head Coach, Tommy Bowden to get fired the next day. Wake and Coach Grobes' staff was getting pretty good at beating teams and getting their head coaches fired. This was the beginning of Dabo Swinney's tenure and the start of Dabo's coaching career at Clemson as a head coach. When KJ got recruited and decided to go to Clemson, KJ would often tell Dabo, "You know you are here because of my dad and Wake" meaning his dad was part of the staff at Wake that got the other head coach fired.

Being a college football coaches wife has taken me to some wonderful schools starting at North Carolina A&T State University (Greensboro, NC), Ohio University (Athens, OH), Wake Forest University (Winston-Salem, NC), Catawba College (Salisbury, NC), University of North Carolina Charlotte (Charlotte, NC), Western Carolina (Cullowhee, NC), and now back to North Carolina A&T State University. As a team wife, our closets hold most of the team colors until we depart. So I have had blue, gold, black, white, purple, grey, and green just for college colors. If you add all the children's high school and college teams, the only color in the rainbow I haven't touched is RED.

AFCWA (American Football Coaches WIVES Association)

AFCWA is a sisterhood of the College Football Coaches Wives Association. We are made up of NFL, D1, D2 on down to High School Coaches wives from all over the world if they come. Every year when the football coaches would have their national convention, the first week of January, Keith would go without me. New into our marriage we didn't start having children until after our third year. I was in graduate school at Ohio University, and really had no true desire to go to the wife's convention until I kept hearing the other wives come back and talk about their adventures. I mentioned going with Keith a few times but grumbles and my interests in going kept falling on deaf ears. Over the next few years, our son KJ was born and Kirstie, our oldest daughter, was now a teenager, but my curiosity didn't stop. My mother-in-law, Mary, agreed to keep the kids but Keith was now totally against me going, but that didn't stop me either. What is this sisterhood and support system you ladies speak of? Who are all these beautiful women in the pictures and newsletters I keep reading about in the AFCWA newsletters and what workshops designed just for ME? I made a decision that I was going to go. The next convention was in Indianapolis, Indiana. One thing about coaching football is because there are at least 10 coaches on a staff, there are possibly 10 new family members (coaches, wives and their families) that you now know in other parts of the United States. One of our former graduate assistant coaches, Ron Antwan and wife Zena, now live in Indianapolis. I called them and had a place to stay. I knew if I found a reasonable flight AND PAID MY MONEY, I was going. I planned it all and didn't let Keith know until the week before. Well, after I told him I was going, the conversation went more like, "You are not going", Keith said. "Yes, I am, I already have my ticket," I said. "Where are you staying?" he asked and for him his argument went downhill. During this time, in the mid-90s cell phones weren't as popular as they are today. I arrived and got settled in and was off to the wives' convention. We have a schedule from the time you come in on Sunday, with opening welcome session, workshops on moving, social media, fashion show, silent auction to raise funds for our scholarship given to wives who are in school, visits to the local children's hospital where the AFCWA makes a huge monetary donation, and our final session of a High Tea. We have had speakers at our luncheon like Lou Holtz (my favorite – Dr Lou), Barbara Bush, Mary Lou Retton and many more. I was like a kid in the candy store, all these wonderful women in the first years, about a hundred or so, but now about double. Some women just come to be with their husbands and get away and don't participate in the convention activities, and others now come as they might be girlfriends or a fiancé, but either way we welcome all and man have we grown.

Well Keith still wasn't happy I was there, but I did start noticing more attention from him that weekend, wasn't sure why. He called the house and most of the conversation was, *"Where you going? Where you been?, Where you at"* ....I know Mrs. Aldrich, from Enloe High School, bad English". My husband was never a jealous, possessive type but when you only have 100+ women in the convention center with over 8000-10,000 men this is not the time to have your wife walking around mad with you. This is not the time to have your wife to be anywhere but beside you or nearby if you know what's good for your marriage. I love the Coaches' convention, for many reasons.

Women Who Lead In Sports

Keith now schedules our trips to the coaches' conventions for the two of us. When we go to the conventions you meet such wonderful coaches and wives. Keith never has to remember anyone's name, everyone there is named "COACH". All you hear all week long is "Hey Coach", "Good to see you Coach" "How you are doing Coach", it is so funny to me. When we go it's like a family reunion and seeing sisters, friends and mentors that we haven't seen in a while. The support system is AMAZING, no one but these ladies, REALLY know what we go through during the football seasons, good and bad.

Most people don't know, but usually as wives, we only get our husbands a few weeks in the summer and a few visits throughout the year. I remember a friend saying, "oh the football season is over now; you get your husband back." Not true. When we were first married, Coaching Season started the first week in August with first years reporting in. In the month of August there were long days and practices two times a day, called "Two a days" …..not many teams have two a days any more, too many athletes complained. Then the football season starts, Sunday- Friday your husband could work 60 hours that week. Fridays are travel days, for away games, and mornings off for home games. Saturday is gameday, so that's all day, depending on gametime, 12 noon, 3pm or 7pm and then mornings off to go to church. Keith and I use to laugh because the time to be in the office on Sundays when we were at Wake Forest was 2pm, well the Head Coach apparently has never been to a black church cause the preaching usually never got started until 1pm so Keith could never stay for the sermon or we had to find another church….we found another church.

After your season is over then it's off to senior recruiting push, during the January and February months. March and April are filled with Spring football practices and the Spring game. In the month of May, we are hopeful to see our husbands on the weekends due to Junior recruitment.

June is for hosting high school football players for camps, two to three weeks and July is the vacation month. The football seasons for us in the ACC, and most big colleges, ran from August until the weekend after Thanksgiving. If you were lucky and won six or more games your team would be invited to at least one extra game called a "Bowl." If not then, the Monday after your season, used to be called "Black Monday ". Black Monday was the Monday after Thanksgiving where if your season didn't go well, depending on what school you were at, or the money your fan base or boosters put up, your head coach (and staff) or what is viewed as the team's weakest links could be fired. Black Monday for football coaches and wives WERE just as popular as "Black Friday" but worse. From December 1st until about March 1st the football coaching hiring and firing shuffle begins. The hiring and firing buzz get so big it makes news on ESPN depending on where you are. Wondering if this is the year, we would get a new job, kind of like being a kid and waiting on your ride to come pick you up to go to a party. Every time a car comes into your neighborhood, you wonder "are they here for me?" ....Ooooo it is stressful. There's now a website that many people troll called www.footballscoop.com where people report behind the scenes gossip (that has a lot of truth to it) on the "ins and outs" of coaching changes. When we were at Ohio University, we were there for seven years. Remember we had the longest losing streak in the nation, but we chipped away, got some really good recruits, ran the really hard to defend, triple option, and built an awesome program in a hard to recruit area, with some really high character kids. Because of this, Coach Grobe started getting some buzz about taking another job. I will give it to Grobe, we called him "Grobie," he always said he won't take a job if he couldn't bring everyone on his staff with him. So for a few years we heard about him interviewing for some jobs, but because the school AD or head hunters would be so strict, he turned them down…. until Wake Forest.

Women Who Lead In Sports

Wake Forest University, in Winston Salem, North Carolina was one of the smallest, next to Duke University in the ACC. Duke and Wake had less than 5,000 students in their undergraduate student population. Most schools in the ACC had over 10-20,000+ students enrolled. Jim Caldwell had just gotten fired and the search was on for a new head coach. Keith and I prayed, and it would have been a seven-year long prayer answered for us. With Keith and I both from North Carolina, Keith is from Maiden, and I from Raleigh, our families are mostly both found in these two cities. Every time we came home for the holidays, family events, once I saw the sign "Welcome to North Carolina" I always asked God to please return us home. If you don't already know, God answers prayers.

Keith and I were at North Carolina A&T State University in Greensboro, North Carolina and he moved to a city 20 minutes from where we left. That's God. When we heard the news, it was again on ESPN. So much happens so quickly behind the scenes with new hires and fires, Grobie hadn't had time to let us know. We have speculated that it was a done deal and even quietly behind the secret chats the OU wives and I had, we made a pack that if we get this job at Wake Forest, we would all get pregnant and have another baby. I laugh at this now, what a thing to wager, but we did it. The next set of Coaches kids were born, Trey, Capri, Maggie, Layne, Maya, Tyler and Jada were all born. So many kids were born that the local newspaper, The Winston-Salem Journal, did a story on how fast our staff was growing.

Recruiting

I tell my grandboys, "College recruiting is a formula, like chemistry. If something is missing out of the mixture, your product is weak". We review this formula almost monthly on our car ride to school. The formula sounds simple but it's not always possible for players to retain. Athletics, Academics, Behavior, Character, and a new one, Social Media is it, do you or your player have the formula?

Women Who Lead In Sports

Let's start with athletics, the freaky-gifted, athletic, talent a player might have. Some have athleticism genetically, some work really hard to get it, but either way only a few have it. Most athletic kids are big, tall and have "good feet" as my husband says. We often look at kids and say, "he has or doesn't have good feet. Bone structure are they skinny, fragile or do they have good solid bone frames is another thing we look for. Often times, even though you are not supposed to do it anymore, you will see a coach hug a player, but really, he is feeling his bones. Then there's the little guy, I love them. They usually aren't as tall or big, but they have to play like their hair is on fire, because they always have something to prove. They are the point guards or the running backs, quick, strong and most of all "have NO FEAR".

One thing my husband would say about recruiting is most people think they as coaches only talk to the high school coach and guidance counselor, not true. He likes to talk to the janitor and cafeteria ladies and ask about the players and how they behave in school. How do they act in the hallways or café when these people are around? Parents don't understand, "If your player is GOOD, they will find you." Parents, you are calling, and politicking is not going to get your child in, unless you have millions you want to donate to the program.

Academics, I would often tell my children when taking them to school, "You have one job, what is that?" They would respond, "to get an education." We as parents sometimes feel like the children's grades should start being "good" in high school, well I don't agree. If you start in elementary with high academics, then it will be the norm by high school. KJ is a smart boy, but he wanted to get lazy in high school. He was at Forsyth Country Day school in Lewisville, NC, known for high academics, he did well. Forsyth was dissolving their football program and we transferred KJ to the local high school, West Forsyth. West Forsyth is also the home of Chris Paul and so many other Winston Salem greats, so Kj thought he was going to dummy down. He tried not to take honors classes and do just enough to get by. Most kids and parents don't realize that honors classes just have a fancy name. The student might get a few more vocabulary words or chapters they have to read but it's not a whole lot different from their normal assignments. The grade they receive will be higher than what is printed, a C is the weight of a B and a B is the weight of an A. Well KJ even thought it was dumb when I told him he was going to apply for the national honors society. I told him, "when a college coach comes in to recruit you, pulls your transcript, and sees National Honor Society stamped on the paper, there is no question in their mind that you will belong at their university."

I understand that some students struggle, but I don't understand the lack of some parental involvement. As a former teacher, I am amazed at how many parents would come to the scrimmage Pee Wee football games but don't come to open houses at the kid's school. I can't understand how the parents can buy their electronic tickets to get into the kid's games but don't go online to check grades, meet with teachers or become more involved in the academics of their students. If they struggle, most teachers will give free tutoring or recommend the student to a tutor. In our household academics OR nothing. When our children were in season of their sport, I loved it because my boys will tell you (my girls didn't have this issue), that if they were late to class, they cut up in class, they didn't turn in their work, I would text or email the coach to "run them, or not start" that goes for academics or behavior.

Behavior is something all my children and grandchildren know …..WE DON'T PLAY with around our house. Being a coach's kid wasn't always easy for the boys, I think it didn't phase my girls much. The boys did a lot on game day with dad's players, went to the camps and lived around dad in the office a lot more. If my boys cut up in school, dad wasn't always around, so I had to step in. Keith handled the discipline mostly but if he was out recruiting, I was his back up. I tell my children all the time, "It's what you do on the field AND off the field you have control over ". You might not have control of the weather, you might struggle to control the people around you, but you have control of your academics and behavior. One of my favorite movies is Glory Road, if you haven't seen it add it to your collection. **Glory Road** is a 2006 Sports movie, based on a true story surrounding the events leading to the 1966 NCAA University Division Basketball Championship. Don Haskins, portrayed by Josh Lucas, head coach of Texas Western College (now known as University of Texas at El Paso or UTEP), coached a team with an all-black starting lineup, a first in NCAA history. Well one of the players from Detroit was cutting up in school, and Big Mama gets word of this all the way up north. Mama rides the greyhound bus and just happens to show up in school to her son's college class. Needless to say, this son wasn't pleased but guess what, mama didn't get any more phone calls. I saw this and had to use it on KJ. He was at Forsyth Country Day school and the Spanish teacher called me. She, like a few others, always talked about how respectful KJ was but she was having a bit of trouble out of him and a few of the other boys. Well, I don't have rights to the others but, I have rights to Keith Jerimiah Henry, so I requested a day where I could come to class. KJ nor the other boys, knew I was coming. I walked in, greeted the teacher by saying, "Buenas Tardes" (Good afternoon) and sat down. Well in this class there were three African American boys, and all of them knew me. One of the white kids looked at the boys and said, "Whose mama is that?" KJ turned to the other two black boys and said, " I don't know, whose mama is that with a smile". I didn't have any more trouble out of KJ in school again.

The other part of behavior my husband always says, "you are who you hang out with". Your friends and your crew speak volumes of who you are. I made it a *must to know* who my children's friends are. I made it *a must to know* their parents, call their parents if they went to their house. I didn't let them stay over on school nights, asked parents if they allowed girls to sleep over or if they had sisters or brothers where would they be? I asked what their policy on alcohol in the home is and if they allowed them to go out, what is their curfew time? Too many parents want to be their children's friend growing up, not us, we are not designed to be their friend, but their parents.

For us behavior had rules:

1. You don't call adults by their first name ie. Ms. Nancy or Brother Pierre

2. The boys, take care of your sisters and mother and ALWAYS be respectful to girls and women around you, never hit a girl.

3. You are to respect your teachers, coaches, elders and family

4. You will not talk while adults were talking, say "excuse me"

5. You will learn to dress nice on game day and church, you act differently when you are dressed nice (no jeans, no tennis shoes etc.). Gameday is a business trip.

6. All children have chores starting at the age of two years old, empty trash, sort the silverware, fold clothes, vacuum, dust or match socks, everyone can do something, make a contribution to the household you live or stay in.

7. Cell phones were collected each night and not allowed in the room by a certain time (9pm school days/11pm weekends), sleep is VERY important

8. Volunteering or being involved in church was a must, God has blessed you, bless others with your time, TIME = LOVE.

9. Behavior even has a lot to do with what is allowed on TV. My kids still talk today about how I wouldn't let them watch SpongeBob. Why? Because he was mean, he was not respectful to his friends, not a good role model.

10. Keep yourself, room and bathroom clean. When you leave to go out of town, always have your area nice for when you return. This is a part of discipline and discipline is a part of behavior.

11. It doesn't take much to say "thank you". When I cook, pick them up or drop them off to practice, if I get their hair cut or even a ride to the dentist office, "Thank you" is always in order. Even an old dying art of writing a "thank you note" was required. If money or a gift card was received, they did not get it until they wrote the card to say thank you.

12. Finally, last but not least we taught them to pray out loud. God says if you deny me on earth, I will deny you in heaven. So, I started them young praying out loud. We always pray out loud, when pulling out the driveway to go on a road trip or at the dinner table.

I would always tell the children that character is how you behave when no one is watching. If you see paper on the ground, do you pick it up or do you leave it? What do you do when no one has asked you to do something? Are you late to practice or first to practice? Do you stay behind and work on your craft or complain because Coach doesn't play you enough?

Recruiting for our household turned to the flip side of a pancake, when you see your husband doing the recruiting now your son is being recruited. I always called recruiting "begging". I would see Keith have chats with players on the phone, write them "letters" I called them, "Love Letters" because you showed the players so much love and attention. Then you checked the newspapers for their scores, or write ups now you have Max Prep or recruiting services and social media. "Time equals love" so if you are spending time trying to get a kid, you are showing them love. For a lot of Keith's recruits, coming from single moms or grandparents that raised them, he had to be patient and show a lot of love. I am thankful that so many players are like our extended family and we still keep in touch with today.

Recruiting for us took a turn with KJ. KJ Henry, is our oldest son who played football, basketball and baseball (until 9th grade), and baseball was a sport his father wanted him so desperately to keep. KJ said, "if Chris Paul can stop in the 9th grade, I'm going to stop in the 9th grade". I really was happy, because I hated baseball; it was too slow, hot, cold, rainy, dusty and boring. So, KJ had decided in his mind, he was going to be an NBA player. He loved basketball, but he didn't work at it. Keith and I kept telling him if you don't put up 300-500 shots a day, work hard in the off season and develop a 3-point shot, he would just be a mid-major, average college basketball player. Now don't get us wrong, we were okay with this. We have told all of our children, "there are four of you, so please try TO GET COLLEGE PAID FOR." KJ was a 6'5, 190 pounds good size thick-kid, played defense well, was an awesome basketball center BUT in mid- high level college basketball, this 6' 5 player is a guard. KJ was not a guard. By the summer of KJ's 10th grade year, ESPN came out with their high school football nation-wide rankings. I didn't know what these were but after my phone started buzzing with all new text messages, I soon found out. KJ was ranked 17th in the nation by ESPN.........Whattt the what??? Then the fall of his junior football season, at West Forsyth High School, he had a game one Friday night where he was playing defense and he grabbed an interception and ran it for an 80-yard touchdown. Keith said, "you are about to start getting your first college football offers soon" and he did. Coach Larry Fedora, from University of North Carolina Tar Heels, called and gave KJ his first D1 football offer. After that, the word got out about this big coach's kid from North Carolina, and the recruiting carnival began.

KJs recruiting started subtly, a few phone calls here, a camp brochure there, but for high school football recruiting, September 15th was "D

Day". "D Day was the first day junior high school players could start being recruited by mail and unlimited phone calls. WOW, did they lower the boom on KJ with all the mail he collected. KJ got so much mail we had to alert our postman and then put a large ice cooler at our mailbox, so all of the new mail could be received. For about two weeks, KJ got posters, letters, pictures, handwritten note cards and some of the most interesting and creative mail we have ever seen. Today, we still have a lot of what was sent but two of the most memorable schools were Clemson University and University of Georgia.

The University of Georgia must have had an art class that they had on payroll, because they sent to the house 100 beautifully drawn, well detailed and colorful handmade note cards. How do I know there were 100 you ask, because each one was numbered, though not received in order on the same day, but 100, nonetheless? At the bottom of the outside of the envelope it would say 43rd reason to come to UGA, 17th reason to come to UGA, 100th reason to come to UGA. If you didn't know the UGAs mascot, school colors, location, the football staff names, the school song, favorite things to do, foods the school offered, about the "Hedges", famous alum, you didn't read any of the 100 note cards that were sent to the house.

Clemson had one of the best social media campaigns online with several different creative postings on every holiday, KJs birthday, but also the posters they sent. It was an election year, so they sent KJ a picture of him, standing at a US presidential podium. They knew education was important to me so they photoshopped his name onto a Clemson University diploma. Clemson also had just one national championship, so they had KJs pictures beside the national championship trophy, they were so creative. Big posters, little trading cards, even puzzles you had to put together, these recruiting measures were crafted well with the player in mind.

Women Who Lead In Sports

Recruiting handwritten cards were received by KJ, myself, his sister, father and grandmother. I now call this recruiting, "stalking" with all this daily constant attention, a good problem to have.

So, some of the protocol of recruiting is talking with coaches on the phone, if you play other sports, they will come to the high school games. We tried to visit campuses for unofficial visits (tours or visits that the PLAYER has to pay for) and then the Official visit which is a two-night three-day visit to campus (where the SCHOOL you visit pays for.) The school can pay for transportation, gas reimbursement or plane fare, food, game tickets and a real orientation and in-depth view of the university and all it has to offer.

Then there are the home visits from the head coaches and staff. During these visits most families cook or have food ordered and the head coach, offense or defensive coordinators and position coaches come in to visit and what Keith calls, to "seal the deal". If they allow you in your home and you eat their food, or if the coaches come and eat your food, they really want you. My most memorable visit was Dabo, head coach of Clemson. I had cooked a great crock pot stew that my sweet aunt Annette in Las Vegas had taught me, Shrimp and Chicken Etouffee. I consulted with my mother-in-law Mary, to plan the perfect side dishes and desserts and a special shipment of Mary's lemonade was sent in. Whenever I cook for someone, I always try to find out if they have an allergy, or a food they don't like, Dabo has neither. He, Coach Brent Venables (now head coach at University of Oklahoma) and Coach Todd Bates came to our home to eat as well. It was a great visit, Dabo talked for almost two hours, non-stop, we loved catching up. Dabo, Keith, KJ and I talked about recruiting, games, players and so many life situations. Dabo was sitting in front of my kitchen window not knowing that our vent register on the floor was broken. Dabo began telling a story and got sooo animated until he –jumped up, pushed his chair back to have the leg get stuck in the floor causing him to fly backwards. OMG, when I tell you how embarrassed I was to see him almost go flying through my back window as he fell out of the chair. Dabo was a great sport and had good athletic genes because he jumped up and didn't miss a word out of his sentence when telling his story. I... wanted ....to..... die.

Now there are rules to this recruiting game and we were NOT a family that was looking to break those rules. Keith is in the college coaching world, and we did not want to have to look over our shoulder or be nervous about a doorbell ringing and just plain wanted to sleep at night; but don't think schools didn't try to be shady. One school offered Keith a college football coaching job with a 6-figure salary. One school, I found out later, gave us a hotel room that we didn't pay for. One school's alumni approached one of our friends, Kelly, and asked her, "how much do I need to put on this check to get that Henry boy here?" We went to another school for an official visit and the head coach kissed me like a dirty uncle "sneak kiss'' on my cheek after he hugged me a little too tight. Today that coach is out of a college and pro job for doing a lot more than "sneaking a kiss." All in all, when KJ finally announced, I was a happy camper because all the recruiting/stalking stopped, but we are thankful.

KJ announced his college decision, December 21, 2017. He wanted to have his announcement with his West Forsyth high school teams, family and with friends around. Most kids put hats on the table and just announce where their next chapter in life will be, this is THEIR day to shine. Some players now do a video announcing their college commitment or on social media sites and are interviewed right after, KJ's announcement was much different. I didn't know until he announced where he was going, I didn't want to know. Why, you asked? Well, I told KJ, and all of my children, "wherever you go WE go". I might have to pack a lunch and drive or jump in an airplane but either way, we are there. Also, sooooo many people were asking me about his decision, and I knew that people would talk, so I didn't want it to leak out. No one can ever say, "I heard that from KJ's mom," where he wanted to go, because it didn't really matter to me. Sure, I had favorites, a team or a coach I wasn't fond of, but it was his choice. Announcement day finally came, we were all backstage at the high school, very nervous. KJ's sisters', Kirstie and Maya, couldn't wait for his announcement so the bag KJ brought was highly guarded but they took a peek. If you want a true tear-jerking moment, go onto Google, type in "KJ Henry Announcement," then click on SBNation.com and get the Kleenex ready. For me it doesn't take much to cry, but KJ shares his announcement with his special-needs assistant football coach, Patrick Murphy. One of the biggest announcements a high school kid can make, and KJ allowed Coach Murphy, on live ESPN to tell the world where "they" were going. This act of love and kindness is a small example of how sweet my son is for others, his family and community.

Clemson University

KJ committed to Clemson, announcing in late December, then after a quick Christmas got ready to play in the All-American Bowl in Florida. As soon as we finished with the bowl, it was off to get him to Clemson University in South Carolina, about two hours away. Being recruited for so long, over a year, then being whisked from games, to interviews, to events, games and then packing for school is a lot.

Clemson and a number of the Power 5 schools is no easy cake walk. Most players go into a deep shock their freshman year because they receive so many honors in high school, when they get to college, they are no longer "the man." Your four and five stars are in the same locker room with other four and five stars. KJ's first decision was to pick a roommate, Trevor Lawrence. Trevor was the top 5-star quarterback in the nation, and they met at a NIKE football event earlier in the year. Trevor was quiet, sweet and such a nice respectable young man. For about half the season, Trevor was able to be just Trevor, but my mother's senses were on. People or fans would wait in their cars outside their dorm rooms or follow them to class for autographs. I was concerned because Clemson was one of the few schools that had open doors and people could just walk in their apartments. Well, KJ, Trevor and a few freshmen like Xavier Thomas were able to just enjoy being a regular college student until Kelly Bryant lost his starting position. When Trevor took the starting position, there was no looking back for the privacy they both once knew.

On the parent side, navigating as a freshman mom was very overwhelming. First housing was impossible, if you did find a hotel it would cost $600-1,200 a night just to stay, so our real estate company invested early in a nearby condo. Next getting to the game, people don't understand, it is not easy. Clemson is hot, parking is not close and not until recently a shuttle bus or golf carts weren't easy to find. Finally, I noticed that it still wasn't easy enjoying the game, for me, nerves set in. I was nervous for KJ and all of his teammates because now, those boys were my boys.

Over the next few years, they were great, we were winning, going to bowls, even winning a national championship. When you win, people love you, but you are only as good as your last game.

I went to all of KJ's home games and most of all his away games. From September to January, on my weekends I wore purple and orange for five seasons. The families that we met are our families and Clemson University embraced KJ with a love that was shown later.

Here are a few words of advice if you have a college athlete in your life:

1. Plan early, we had to schedule our hotel rooms, or Airbnb the very first week the schedule came out. My first choice is an Airbnb; I can cook, wash clothes, and get more room for less.

2. As a parent, going early to everything, traffic, weather, other sports or entertainment activities in the nearby cities can cause you to miss something good.

3. Pack your own food and water in your clear bags. Most people don't know that "for medical reasons'' you can have your own food. This food strategy is good if you are vegan, diabetic, or have other health issues. There have been about five times I have been to a stadium and they have run out of water. Most venues will allow you to bring one bottle of unopened water to the game. I always pack a salad from the grocery store, a piece of chicken, yogurt or a few health bars. If I ate at the concession stands every time I went to my husband or kids game, in the past 30 years, I would be 400 pounds.

4. If your player gets free tickets, then take care of family first or people who have supported your child along the way. While at Clemson, we felt that the opening game day experience, running down the hill, was the best 25 seconds of college football. We tried to bless at least one new family or friend a week with a free ticket for people who have never been. This is a MUST see, add to your bucket list, if you love college football.

5. Friends and Family don't assume now that this player gets a free ticket or two you are entitled to receive these tickets every week. Ticketmaster, Stubhub, Geek Seat all have discounted tickets for you to enjoy. This goes for game tickets AND your parking tickets.

6. Parents of a player, plan ahead with your guest, be strategic in who you invite, they are a representation of you, as you sit around other players' families and other coaching staff members. If Pookie and Ray Ray are known to be late to

events, OR show up drunk or smelling like weed, guests who will be the topic at Monday morning football staff meeting.

7. Check the weather the week and days before the game. Outside sports, this is KEY! In South Carolina the heat is NOT the same heat in other parts of the country. If your 85-year-old family member wants to come to the 12-noon game in September, in Clemson, South Carolina, you might want to reconsider their attendance unless you want to be at Urgent care by kick off.

8. Parents, your social media is not your own anymore. What you post will be followed by your players, college team, coaches, staff and fans. Post wisely.

9. Parents enjoy and players enjoy, but just know this short-lived fame is good and not always so good. People will ask some of the most outlandish requests of you and your player. Just, smile and focus on how you respond.

10. Support is key, parents and players, find a mentor. Find someone who you can vent to in a confidential way. Players have so many college mental health services, campus ministries, and coaches. Parents talk to a mature and seasoned parent in the team family. You are going to have questions about, "why isn't my child getting playing time?"

11. "What do we do because our player is injured or has COVID, flu, or sickness?" "How do I best navigate this situation during the season?"

Being a female Ref

After years of playing basketball, in high school, college club and pick up ball with the men at the Y, I knew my body couldn't stay in that environment and not get injured. My husband, in his early 40s came and played pick up ball with me at the Y and played so hard he tore his Achilles heel and had to have surgery. I wanted to stay in the game and for a long time I wanted to ref, I just either was too afraid or didn't know what to do. One day, Keith and I were talking to someone about sports and Keith said he was going to start reffing basketball. I said to myself, "not before me" and I set off to find my way. At the young age of 40 years old, I started. Now being a female ref was rare then and still rare now. In the year 2010, I came in. There were only five females out of 25 males in our rookie class. Females move up quicker they told us, and my classmate did. Out of the five, two of them are now reffing on the college level and three of us are still at it. In our Winston Salem association, there were only 10-12 females out of over 100 male refs, roughly 10 percent. Being a female ref or coach in a male dominated sport is extremely hard that is why I always commend the female refs I see in the NFL, NBA and even, third year, Assistant Coach Jennifer King who is a female Assistant football coach for the Washington Commanders.

How did you start reffing people who often ask me? Well, it's simple, I walked up to a ref after a game and asked, who books you and how do I get started? Wow, did I learn a lot that day. Each sport has a season, the main sports are football, basketball, volleyball, baseball, track and softball. Now more sports are coming up, field hockey, swimming, tennis and even pickleball need refs too. To be a basketball ref we ALL have to take classes in the fall. You can ref three years or 25 years we all have to attend our local meetings AND the statewide meeting. When I first started 14 years ago, it was harder and more political to get in, to be a basketball ref, and get games, a good ole boys' network. But if you are good, organized, look professional and are dependable you will get games. But, did I find that female refs became in high demand for girls' games and girls' tournaments. Early on, I found that reffing varsity high school games, 3-man, and college games were not in the cards for me. That's the next question that I am often asked, "what level do you ref or do you do college reffing?". Well the answer is "No". No, because of a few reasons, one I have four children and ALL of them have played and now the youngest is still playing high school varsity basketball, I absolutely love coming to my children and grandboys games. Secondly, the varsity games are late, can go into overtime, have more fights and the pay is about $10 more………. "not worth it". His high school varsity games only benefit me as it is a 3-man crew, meaning there are three of us out there on the court rather than two. For middle school, JV and AAU basketball most games are only 2-man, we work a lot harder. The other reason is if you are a college ref, you have to be at the gyms sometime four hours before a game, because of traffic. You sometimes have to leave home a day before or go through a lot of arrangements just to make it on the court. I had to ask myself, "What is my goal as a ref?" My goal is simple, I want to show girls and African American girls there's a female ref. I want to help teach the game from the court and encourage the players from the baseline. I want to give back to my community, and I do that by giving free basketball workshops called, Basketball 101. I make it clear to all my booking agents that I only want middle school and JV. I call JV the stallions, so I can help encourage the young people and then go out the door to do books or volunteer at my children's game. I also give classes on doing scores to the young people and show them that doing the book and reffing is a great side hustle. Lastly, I do get paid to exercise, and as much as I like to eat, this helps.

Finally, I am asked how much we get paid. Well before I give you the amounts just know; we definitely don't do it for the money. I would often try to go to the ref where my children or grandchildren were playing. This was sometimes very risky for me because these gyms are becoming a battle ground on the court and for parents off the court. But I figured if I save the $20-$40 entry fee and go make $20-$30 a game, it was worth my gas, and paying for our meals. So, here's the breakdown

Women Who Lead In Sports

YMCA pays $10-15 a game – (I'm not working these games, but a great place for a kid to start or a rookie who wants to get some court time)

When you work for a booking agent, in the state of North Carolina you are paid a 2024 state rate:

Varsity – per game - 3 refs	$77
Varsity double header - 3 refs (girls and boys)	$154
JV per game - 2 refs	$71
JV double header 2 refs	$142
Tournaments 1 game	$88
Tournaments – double header	$176
State Playoffs round 3-5	$104.50
State Finals	$110
AAU or off-season tournaments	$20-$35 a game

Some might think it's a lot of money, as refs, we know it's not enough for what we endure. Since COVID, we have lost a lot of refs due to the crazy players, crazy coaches and we are not going to leave out the crazy parents. Before we work one game we have to pay for our uniforms, shoes, booking fees and that doesn't include gas and food. Here's what an estimated cost is just to suit us out for one basketball game.

State Association fee $100 (can vary from state to state)

HS Booking Fee $75-150 (depending on who or what level you work for)

Women Who Lead In Sports

Pants (no loops black) $50-$60 and you have to get them hemmed, each

Stripped White Shirt $50 each

Stripped Grey Shirt $50 each

Ref Jacket $65 each

Whistle $7 each

Mask $10 (we had to wear during COVID)

Compression Shorts $20-$40 each

Sports Bra $50 (the girls have to be TIGHT) each

Shoes (must be all black) $100-$250 my favorite are Brooks

Socks (must be all black) $20 a pack

What I have learned, we can referee year-round if you want. With all the sports named above this is some people's full-time or supplement your retirement job. We can referee basketball or a lot of sports like volleyball almost 45-50 weeks out of the year. You need to love the sport you are reffing. I love basketball, I like volleyball, because of the wear and tear of basketball I am now picking up volleyball. Volleyball has less movement on my boy and less stress from parents and coaches. In the years I have referred to, I have seen a lot of fights, parents and coaches thrown out and our overall safety level decreased. Did you know if you hit a ref it is a FELONY, most don't realize that? I have even learned my physical limits, during weekend tournaments I now will do no more than four games. If the booking agent has a need, someone didn't show or someone is late I will fill in, but I am NOT a fan of much more. Some refs will call 8, 10, 12 games in a day, or in a row......that's crazy. I need my knees too bad and don't ever want to have a NEED for that much money anyway.

Women Who Lead In Sports

And since the incident in Greensboro, I have also learned the hard way to say "NO".

I learned to say "No" and know my limits after my March 2022 tournament in Greensboro, North Carolina. I was still in the rookie stage of my career and I accepted a job to ref High School, 2-man showcase tournament (Stallions). I was in an upstairs gym, the only female ref, and the gym had bathrooms downstairs. I had to walk/run over three courts, down two flights of stairs and across the first floor YMCA just to use the women's bathroom. I was supposed to have four games but soon four turned into six and six turned into eight. The last three games I was refereeing by myself because several older seasoned refs said, "hell nah we getting out of here". The young girl at the table that was taking the score, she often fell asleep, literally, while doing the clock or between the five minutes before the next game. All I remember, I was exhausted, but I didn't want to leave the players hanging. I didn't want the person putting on the tournament down and I felt obligated to help out. Unfortunately, my body did not comply, so I soon stopped running and had to referee, first leaning up against a wall, and later sat down in a folding chair. Well with cameras in hand and pictures and videos now a thing, someone took a picture and video and posted it online. The story title read, "Referee at regional showcase takes laziness to new level, calls games from midcourt folding chair"….. Whattttt? and Yahoo Sports picked it up and ran with it. I made national, online headlines.

My cousin in California, Claudia, called me and said, "did you recently ref in Greensboro?" I said "Yes". "Did you ref basketball from a folding chair?" she said. I then gave a long gasping pause……." Yes." "Well you have been named one of the laziest refs and it just popped up on my Yahoo Sports feed".   I cried!!! I just wanted to crawl up under a rock and simply DIE!!

Women Who Lead In Sports

I'm a NFL Mom

"I'm an NFL Mom" one mom said during the 2023 football draft this year. Those words play over and over sometimes in my head, but like KJ said in his recent interview with Commander's Podcast, "Next Man UP" all of this NFL stuff, really hasn't hit me yet. Seven months after the draft and I still can't believe we have made it to the NFL, let me tell you why.

So KJ's journey to be out front or have his name being called over the loudspeaker at the Clemson stadium, as he tackles or sacks the quarterback, hasn't always come easy to him. At Clemson he started out as a freshman playing behind first round teammates like Dexter Lawrence (or Sexy Dex) who is now a starter for the New York Giants and another teammate, Christian Wilkins, who is now starting for the Miami Dolphins. KJ's rookie season at Clemson soon showed him he needed more time to mature. Most recruits at a Power 5 school take it hard when a coach tells them they are going to be "redshirted" (held back from playing this year) but not KJ. See right now in college football, you can play up to three games and then redshirt a player, so most coaches allow the freshman to play and then decide if they need more time to develop. Develop means lifting weights, learning the football playbook more, maturing socially, sharpening interviewing skills and just plain getting better. So, KJ was the first player to go into Dabo's office and tell him, "I want to redshirt myself this season". Dabo was blown away. "If you need me to come out of the redshirt because someone gets injured or it's not helping the team, I will come back out, but I want to redshirt" KJ said. Even today, Dabo talks about KJs maturity and says what was best for him.

KJ was reclassed in high school, and redshirted at Clemson, he had an extra COVID year added to his college years and even though it only took him three years to do his undergraduate degree, and one year to do his masters, he spent five years at Clemson. I tell everyone the final year he took "Underwater basket weaving 101". He didn't have the most traditional route to the Pros, but when all of his friends and teammates left in middle school, when he reclassed, and went on to high school I told him then, and I tell him now, "your path is YOUR path." Your Grandma Mary named you Jeremiah for a reason, in the bible, Jeremiah 29:11 says, "for I know the plans I have for you, plans to prosper you and not harm you (NIV). I keep those words in front of our conversations, even today.

Now even though KJ spent five years playing at Clemson, most of those years, he was best known as what I called, the "Hype Man". At the beginning of the game and when Clemson needed the crowd to get loud, KJ was running to the student section, jumping up and down and getting the crowd "Hyped." KJ played, then KJ started and his patience paid off as he grew into more playing time, more tackles and sacks, but he really stood out his fifth season, this was his best year. If you read his final season bio, it talks about 13.5 sacks, four fumble recoveries etc. but I am most proud of so much more. He was voted a permanent team captain, he received the PAW Journey Man of the year award, two time all academic ACC selection, receiving The Tim Bourrett award (recognizing the player who best represents himself, his teammates and Clemson University in the media) …..and the kind heart he has, the community service and helping his father and others raise money for his kidney transplant through the Help Hope Live organization.

OK, back to the NFL journey, so after KJs final football season was over, we had to interview sports agents. The financial planners and money management people came out of the wood work too. Your son's information and parents' names and numbers might as well be put on a billboard because the phone calls get so bad, some parents and players usually change their cell phone numbers during this time. Depending on the level you are projected to get drafted, first, second, third round depends on how much the agents will invest in you. Even though the agents might tell you, "I will pay to send you to work out,

Women Who Lead In Sports

I will pay for your housing while you are working out, I will pay for your car, food etc." None of this is FREE! The sports agents invest in you, but they have got to get something back on their investment. KJ got a great agent, I won't go into details but just remember EVERYTHING is negotiable. I'm sure KJ was pretty easy with his request, because from what was told to us, there are some real high and crazy demands out there.

Next, we needed to plan a draft party, some can do big parties at a venue or their house, or if you are really blessed to be considered a first round draft pick, you and your family with your college coaches can go to the city which is hosting the NFL draft.

So, I asked KJ what do you want to do on draft day? KJ said he wanted to be with family, he wanted it to be at home, but he didn't want people around him until he got drafted and God heard his prayers.

Draft Day was the 88th annual meeting of the National Football League, held in Kansas City, Missouri, from April 27-29th, 2023. Day 1 the first round of the draft KJ, sat at home with Keith, me and Isaiah. We loved watching his teammates, Myles Murphy go 28th to the Cincinnati Bengals and Bryan Bresee was 29th to the New Orleans Saints, we were so happy and proud of these boys, they have worked so hard.

Day 2 starts the second and third rounds of the draft and on this day names are called a little quicker. On Day 2, KJ's younger brother had to leave to go play for his AAU team CP3 in Arizona. It was hard to get Isaiah out the door that day because he wanted to be there for KJ but his team only had six players (including him) to play on the biggest high school stage in America, EYBL Nike basketball circuit, so he had to go. On this day, KJ watched his other team mate, Trenton Simpson go to the third round to the Baltimore Ravens, nerves were high! We stayed up and watched the Friday names be called for what seemed like hours, KJ's phone didn't ring. We went to bed that night, and I slept kind of restlessly. I woke up on Saturday and the words "Redskins" came to my mind. See, my grandmother, Ordee, had the gifts of prophecy, dreams that would tell her about things, and I have it too. So, I got up and wrote the name on a card and put it on my nightstand. Out of 32 football teams, this was the only name I say. I told KJ several things over the course of the month and if I really analyzed the things, I said to him it would have told me where he was going. I said to him, "watch you gonna end up going to one of our family's teams (Eagles, Washington Commanders, Panthers, Broncos, Seahawks, Cowboys). I told him, you will go to a team where someone has coached you or you grew up and the coach knew you. We had a few coaches that were in the NFL that knew KJ from one college team or another. Then finally, I told him, "Watch, you will get a call when your lil' brother is on the basketball court and when gets done playing, someone will tell him 'your brother just got drafted to the……..'. Can you believe that ALL of these statements became true?

Day 3, the draft picks are being called even faster. My "tom boy" at heart kicked in and I really wanted to put my hair up in a ponytail and put on sweatpants and just hide away somewhere in my happy place but I knew there would be tons of video and pictures done…….We PRAY today. It was about noontime and the caterer and family who wanted to help arrived. I made sure everyone stayed outside, the last thing we wanted was a lot of people around, looking at the TV, then looking at KJ, looking at his phone activity, looking at KJ, LOOKING at the TV, Looking at KJ. We had Keith, my father Claude, KJ's two sisters Kirstie and Maya, his sports agent Scott, his wife Courtney, their son and myself. We wanted to stay positive, prayerful for the RIGHT team and phone call. KJ's phone rang, and it was a team that had a coach on it that knew KJ when he was growing up. They said, "we are really fighting for you in the war room" but his name was never called. Isaiah was playing in Arizona on Day 3 and his game was about to start. KJ was looking at his game on the iPad and in between draft picks fussing at the CP3 team and his brother was a great distraction. It was about 2 pm now, a few more people for the draft party started to arrive early, so outside is where they had to sit until the "call" was received. I got hungry, so I warmed some leftovers and as soon as the microwave timer went off, KJ said, "mom what cha gotta eat" I had to laugh, I didn't think he was hungry but I guess hunger won over nerves today, so I handed him my plate. As soon as he finished eating and the microwave timer went off again, I saw him pick up the phone, so I grabbed my phone to record and heard sister Maya start weeping loudly. "Yes, sir Coach, send the playbook my way, I'm ready" and as soon as he hung up the room was dead silent, KJ turned and said, "Washington Commanders' '. Wow, screams, tears and nothing but pure JOY rang the room. Maya was crying, my 82-year father had tears in his eyes, I of course was bawling, Kirstie was full of hugs, Scott dabbed him up and gave a big hug and the happiest was his father. "MY BOY" the grip-hug, tears, and biggest smile on Keith's face, I have ever seen. I tell people all the time, I don't think I have ever made this man this happy. More family members arrived, pictures and videos were taken. I told our friend Kelly to go upstairs and get the card off my nightstand. I told the family that God gave me a dream and I wrote down on a random thank you card on my nightstand what God said. "Ahhhhhhh" Kelly screamed, "No way" she said coming down the steps. No one could believe that the card read, "Redskins' ' on it. The Clemson reporter that was there took pictures of it and wrote it in his story. Keith got missing for a few minutes, he came downstairs wearing Jeremiah Trotter's Washington Redskins jersey and his Redskins ball cap. He wasted no time getting into his favorite NFL team gear. The irony is that the retired Redskin, Jeremiah Trotter's son, was also KJ's Clemson teammate and his sweet, beautiful wife Tammy, who passed during the season, was my dear friend.

Women Who Lead In Sports

The Washington Commanders traded up to get KJ in the fifth round, he went to his father's favorite team, one of the coaches on the Washington staff, Steve Russ, was a football coach with us at Wake Forest University, he is in a city where family is, and he was a short plane ride or driving distance from home. What a GREAT draft day celebration day it was. What a thankful family we are. See unlike when you are being recruited for college sports, then you have choices. Everyone loves you, or they act like they do, and want you in the locker room. Well, when you go pro, you are now fighting grown ass men for their job. This man, who has a wife, two kids, and one on the way. I don't want a rookie coming into the locker room to steal their job. The NFL locker rooms are nowhere near as welcoming as college. The family connections we make in college, "your son is my son," is not the same in the NFL. The NFL stands for "Not For Long" and this business is just that, A BUSINESS. So instead of knowing mothers on our current NFL team, I still communicate with other moms on the National NFL roster that were KJs teammates like Amanda Lawrence (Trevor Lawrence's KJ's roommate, mom Jacksonville Jaguars), Breyone Murphy (Myles Murphy's mom Cincinnati Bengals, Dionna Ford, (Trenton Simpson's mom Baltimore Ravens). These ladies, we compare notes, vent, pray for our sons, laugh and cry over all that we go through and what to expect (or no longer expect) as NFL moms.

If you are lucky to have a school like Clemson, to help prepare the parents for college football parenting journey, you are blessed, but there is NO or very little prep for what you get into for the NFL. Our team at Clemson is and was a family. I was a team mom for about four of the five years KJ was there, making sure that each new parent felt welcomed. I called and talked to almost all newcomers and did workshops on navigating "game day", we were a close-knit family. On the NFL level, forget it, remember this is a business. Some of our moms had a hard time adjusting to this, other parents are not very friendly. They think out of 80 plus players that start out in the pre-season, by September your son probably won't make the 53-man roster. Most families viewed this as a reason for not getting too close with one another. Now, the Commanders are a rare gem, with having a "Player Development staff." They do zoom workshops for us, on navigating game day, injury protocol, who to contact for game day issues or safety, just to name a few.

In college, all the players' families sit together, no tickets are paid for, if you sit in the parent section; all tickets were compliments of the school. In the pros, you pay for your tickets, they do sit us in the same section but the best advice I heard from one seasoned NFL mom was "to purchase my own tickets and go sit on the other side of the stadium." Why did she say this, you ask? Well, the NFL fans already know what section is the "family section" and they love your player one day or can hate him the next. Being a coach's wife trained me well for this "what have you done for me lately" attitude but, not all people have had this course.

So, let's review, the player, after their college bowl, if they have one, declares for the draft. This is a verbal announcement either done by video or a post on social media. Then you interview or finalize negotiations to narrow down an agent. You decide if you need a financial planner or money manager immediately, so much to decide in a short amount of time, then your player is off to work out. The work out areas are places like California, Floridia, Atlanta or Arizona, somewhere warm is where most prefer. Then if you are mid to high projections for the draft the agent may or may not pay for your housing, food, rent a car etc. The player works out just about six days a week. If he is coming off of an injury, recovery is on the menu as well. For KJ, he went to Florida, his agent Scott was great, he knew that seeing KJ was important to us and understood the bigger picture. Scott is accessible by text or phone calls almost any time of day. Scott is now family and we love him like a relative, this is how having an agent should be. If we have a question, no matter how big or small, he always responds to us in a timely fashion.

Women Who Lead In Sports

After the draft, depending which round and where you are drafted, you might have to go the day after your name is called to do media day with your new NFL team. For KJ, fifth round, he did his interviews by zoom. Technology is wonderful. Then off to rookie camp, but each team is different. Weeks of living in a hotel, eating food that you aren't always used to, and now living in a strange city gets hard for the NFL guys. YES, NFL is exciting but the human side and homesickness, can, and is a "thing" for a lot of them. The stress of making the 53-man roster is the next thing on their mind. When KJ saw his name on the Commanders roster, in early September, we all celebrated like it was draft day all over again.

Finding housing, getting moved in and purchasing or renting furniture can be hard for the guys, especially if you are not knowledgeable, or unorganized, if you don't have a manager or a team "player development" person, (which most don't) then you are on your own. For KJ, I am that person, "Momanger " my cousin Karen calls me. The first "momanger" assignment was to inform all friends and family that there are no more "FREE game day tickets" to a NFL football game. In college, we got 4-6 free tickets and we could beg the families on the roster who might not use their tickets for theirs, but the Pros are different. Friendly reminder, THIS IS A BUSINESS!! Each player in the pros gets two free HOME tickets, that's it. After that KJ would have to take the purchase of a ticket out of his checks and most don't realize they don't make very much. The away tickets are even worse, the tickets the away teams offer our fans are so high up in the stadium you might see angels flying around you.

Today, as I am writing this chapter, KJ has been a rookie in the NFL for the Washington Commanders for three months now. He started out in his first eight weeks inactive, not dressing out for games but practicing and traveling to the games. This is kind of like being on the practice squad, not playing in regular games, but still getting normal pay as if he is on the field. I didn't mind this at all, because playing in football games is like being in a car wreck every week.

Women Who Lead In Sports

Unless you are the kicker, you usually come out cut, bruised and pray for no injuries every game day.

Half way through KJs rookie season, Week 9, The New England Patriots game, KJ was up, dressing out now to play because two of his defensive teammates, Chase Young and Montez Sweat just got traded. KJ was in the game, my nerves were shot, praying and clutching my hands as I am deeply gazing at the TV for KJs every move, I couldn't rest. KJ came around the offensive lineman to make a beautiful sack, and the ball came out…… .a sack and a fumble….. wow his first sack of the season, during his first REAL game of the season. Wait, what all these yellow flags come out, what for I wonder? The referee goes to his microphone attached to his head, "personal foul, roughing the passer, penalty on defense #55, 15 yards, first down." I screamed all over the house, my phone kept vibrating with so many friends and family fussing and cussing from afar; no one could believe this call was truly happening. KJ went from the

inactive list, to the top story in sports all week long. Our pastor, Bishop Mack (and so many ministers) preach about Matthew 20:16, "So the last will be first and first will be last." I can't tell you how many times I have told KJ this about how God has put this banner over his life. KJ has been in the back of the line, waiting patiently for his chance, and now at the front of the line.

Now with this penalty, unlike college, the player can be fined (a financial bill). NFL players can be fined for being late to meetings, missing public/private required events, or workouts, and even penalties. The Team, they just simply send you an invoice letting you know that your fine was taken out of your paycheck. I knew this but I didn't know it could be UP TO a $40,000 fine. Hold up wait, do these people not know, he is still *ballin* on a budget? Fortunately, one of KJ's teammates (thank you nice young man, you know who you are) said he would pay it if he had to. Your NFL team can appeal these or pay them as well, as the Commanders said they would if they

Women Who Lead In Sports

had to. A week later, The Commanders received a letter stating that KJ would NOT be fined and "we, the NFL, apologize because we made the wrong call." As a ref myself, I understand we are all human and are not perfect. As a mother, my heart broke for KJ because he can't get that credit for a sack and fumble back, but God says, "give praise for ALL things" so we are still thankful. Even at press time, I still don't feel any different but sometimes the people who approach me or recognize me soon slap me back into my senses that I am an NFL Mom.

God says, in James 4:2 "we have not, because we ask not". I always said that if any of my children made it "BIG" I don't want a car, don't buy me a house, I don't want a Superbowl Campbell Chunky soup commercial or shout "I'm going to Disney," I want to do a "Tide" laundry detergent commercial so I can get a "lifetime supply" of Tide pods. The commercial would go like this, our oldest daughter Kirstie, a first responder, in her nursing outfit, husband Keith in his coaching outfit, KJ in his NFL football uniform, Maya as a college student, Isaiah in his college basketball uniform, and me in my basketball referee uniform (not including all the practice and workout clothes we wash) and let people know that I use Tide to clean all of these uniforms clean, to keep our family going every day. So, if anyone reading this book has connections to "Tide" please help this Sports, NFL Mom and Coaches' wife out! ☺ Thank you!

The African proverbs speak of a village that helps raise the children. Being a sports mom, basketball ref and coaches' wife is never easy without a good village. Grandparents, Grandma Mary and Papa Charles, Papa Claude and Grandma Dee and Great-Grandma Alma.... Thank you.

To those at Shiloh Baptist Church, Union Baptist Church for having wonderful youth activities and church mothers and fathers to help with vacation bible school, youth choir, youth usher board, after school tutoring programs and so many prayers.... Thank you!

Women Who Lead In Sports

Neighbors like Ms. Nancy and Mr. Dave, Uncle Johnny and Aunt Dawn, who helped pick up or drop off my tribe at sporting events, played in the snow on Kingsbridge or played basketball with the children, fed them .... Thank you.

God parents Kathy and Donald, Aunts and Uncles Joe, Heather, Trey, Lori, Al, Pessie, Sandy, Aunt Gloria, cousins Asia and Deon for coming to games especially when we couldn't be there, so the children would know that they had someone to support them…. Thank You!

To Jamma, Kelly, Aida, Tammy, Mary who were there with food, a house to spend the night with their children or the rod of correction (the spoon) when the boys needed it….. Thank You!

To the American College Football Coaches Wives, and wives of each of the staff we were a part of, too many sisters to name, the extended family we have, who gave me an outlet of support, to vent and mentor others like me, a sisterhood… Thank You.

To ALL the coaches that had one of the four of the "Henry Children" have played for, YMCA ball, AAU, (basketball, football, volleyball, soccer, track, baseball) school ball for picking up my children or dropping them home (because I was doing the same with another one), making sure they were fed or kept us posted on the game situations, or just taking the time to "Coach" Thank You! If you are reading this and you feel forgotten, just know we are "thankful" for you too.

Finally, but most importantly, THANK YOU GOD for allowing me and our family to be able to do the things we love the most, being involved in sports. Thank you for blessing us, thank you for keeping us safe, healthy and prosperous. To GOD be the Glory!

About Nicole Trotter Henry

Nicole Trotter Henry is a College Football coach's wife, mother to four athletes, and grandmother to two more. Native of Raleigh, North Carolina she played high school basketball and stayed in the game by playing pick-up ball with greats, like Chris Paul and Rusty LaRue but growing up it bothered her she "never saw a female basketball referee" until adulthood. Because of this Henry became a basketball/volleyball referee and female ref recruiter. Henry married her college sweetheart Keith, who was a football coach at North Carolina A&T State University.

Being a Coach's wife has its ups and down, being a referee is no cake walk but as the children grew so did their own D1 recruitment. Nicole's oldest son, KJ Henry was a 5-star recruit ranked #6 nationally for 2018 football class (ESPN), committing to Clemson University, now playing in the NFL for the Washington Commanders. My youngest son, Isaiah Henry, is currently a 4-star nationally ranked high school basketball recruit.

Thank you for taking a look inside Henry's Sports World……

Women Who Lead In Sports

Special Acknowledgment

DeLores "Dee" Green Todd

WOMEN WHO LEAD IN SPORTS
Special Acknowledgement: DeLores "Dee" Green Todd

Barrier Breaking Firsts | DeLores "Dee" Green Todd

DeLores "Dee" Green Todd, a Camden, NJ, native, is a hidden gem in her community. From being a barrier-breaking first in many of her professional endeavors to inspiring an industry in ways she could not have imagined; Green Todd is truly a phenomenon.

Born in Washington, D.C. on February 29th, 1948, the leap year baby grew up a middle child, flanked by an older brother, Lonnie, and a younger brother, Juan. She likes to joke and tell people she's technically only eighteen years old (if only counting the times we actually saw February 29th).

As a young athlete, Green Todd was often limited to intramural competition because Title IX had not yet become law. Title IX requires educational institutions to reward male and female athletes equally and ensures the prevention of discrimination in access to sports facilities, training centers, equipment, and other supports provided to sports programs. Until the passing of this federal civil rights law in 1972, there was no legal requirement of equal sports access and support for women.

Green Todd did enjoy cheerleading. "I was a cheerleader growing up. I cheered all four years at Winston-Salem [University] for basketball and football. I became a captain my freshman year and [still to] this day, I'm the only four-year captain," she proclaimed.

Women Who Lead In Sports

Green Todd went on to earn a master's degree in Human Relations & Psychotherapy and pledged Delta Sigma Theta Sorority at Northwestern University. After college, she taught physical education and coached girls' basketball, cheerleading and track at two high schools. While still teaching at one of them, a friend who owned a modeling agency encouraged Green Todd to start modeling. So she auditioned and landed a McDonald's modeling gig. As her portfolio grew, she worked with Jet and Ebony magazines, Dr. Scholl's and Fashion Fair cosmetics and other companies.

In 1980, when the United States boycotted the Olympics, Kellogg tapped Green Todd to grace the cover of their Corn Flakes box. The model, educator, athlete and coach was the first Black woman to do so. She did not initially recognize the significance of the cover photo until she learned the cereal boxes were flying off of shelves and people wanted her autograph. "It's the biggest thing I've ever done in terms of publicity. Every time the boxes would restock, it would sell out, and people would ask me to autograph their cereal boxes," said Green Todd.

Green Todd is a woman of many firsts. She was the first African American woman to coach at Northwestern University. When named track coach at Georgia Tech in 1985, she became the first African American coach in any sport in the Atlantic Coast Conference (ACC). In 1988 she became the first woman and the first African American to serve as assistant commissioner of the ACC. In 2005, she became North Carolina A&T University's first woman athletic director. She broke barriers coaching at Northwestern University and Georgia Tech, paving a path for other women in sports.

Along the way, Green Todd led advances in women's sports, convincing the NCAA to staff women's basketball with the same number of officials as men's roundball. She successfully championed live television coverage of women's college basketball rather than recording them for playback later.

"Women's basketball was a growing sport, but nobody was able to [notice] it because the conferences wouldn't invest money in it. Equity was the main reason. It just made sense to me and I wanted to help do the right thing," she said.

Delores Green Todd has long believed in inspiring people to make a way for others as she did for them. "It's hard to be what you can't see, so be an example.' I came up with that quote myself, and I always say it because [growing up] I didn't see the example, so I became it," said Green Todd.

She recently finished a six-year term on the Board of Legal Specialization in North Carolina. After retiring, the former track standout accepted a job coaching track at Heritage High School in Wake Forest, NC. There, this trailblazer continues sharing her invaluable experience and insight with another generation of athletes.

In 1995, Dee Todd became the first woman of color to serve as NACWAA (National Association of Collegiate Women Athletic Administrators) president. Dee's time as president saw growth in membership, increased sponsorship, a national search for a full-time executive director, and a "strengthened voice among the ranks of other national associations."

During her presidency, Dee led by her words "We can make our dreams and those of the women who paved the way before us, a reality. WE are Women in Athletics, WE are survivors, WE should strive to share our experiences with each other. WE must instill the need for hard work, honesty, and determination."

After earning a bachelor's degree from Winston-Salem State University and a master's degree from Governors State University,

Women Who Lead In Sports

Dee worked as a teacher and track and field coach at the high school level. Nine years later, Dee was named the first full-time track and field and cross-country coach at Northwestern University, marking the first woman of color head coach in the history of the university. Three years later, she was named Big 10 Cross Country Coach of the Year.

Dee became the head track and field and cross-country coach at Georgia Tech in 1985, again etching history as the first ACC African American head coach. Two years later, she was named the ACC Track Coach of the Year. In 1980, Dee became the first African American female to appear on a box of Kellogg's Corn Flakes.

Dee chaired the United States Olympic Committee, Minorities in Sports Task Force and was the co-founder of the Project Gold leadership class. Many members of the Project Gold classes are successful athletic, political, and community leaders today.

In 1988, Dee became the first female and the first minority to serve as the assistant commissioner of the Atlantic Coast Conference. For 12 years, Dee oversaw the growth of women's basketball and several other sports in the ACC. In 1994, Dee and her SEC counterpart, Pat Wall, led the nation to drive three-person officiating for women's basketball. She was also the first female to serve on the NCAA Division I Baseball Committee. After 17 years at a conference office, Dee became North Carolina A&T State University's first female athletic director. After 50-plus years in the industry, Dee remains active through her retirement with intercollegiate athletics, Speaker on domestic violence and sexual assault prevention, and coaching boys and girls at the high school level, she also serves as a NCAA Baseball Site Rep for Regionals and Super Regionals.

Dee is currently living close to her family in Raleigh, NC Her son Stuart and his wife Charmion are the parents of her grandchildren Mia (14) and Michael Todd (10) who are the joys of her life!

About the Visionary

Dr. Sharon H. Porter

Dr. Sharon H. Porter (Dr. Sharon) is an award-winning educator, best-selling author and publisher, dynamic host, renowned for her multifaceted contributions to education, media, and leadership. As the President of SHP Enterprise, she oversees the operations of Perfect Time SHP LLC, a prominent Book Publishing Firm, SHP Media and Broadcasting, which encompasses the impactful Vision & Purpose LifeStyle Magazine and Media, LLC, and Leadership SHP, a premier coaching and mentorship platform dedicated to developing the next generation of school leaders. Through the New Principal RoundTable (NPR) and the Aspiring Principal Leadership Academy (APLA).

A prominent figure in the media landscape, Dr. Sharon is the owner and Editor-In-Chief of Vision & Purpose LifeStyle Magazine and Media. Additionally, she captivates audiences as the host of The I Am Dr. Sharon Show, showcasing her expertise and engaging interviews. Her influence extends to her role as a NAESP Center for Diversity Fellow with the National Association of Education Principals

Dr. Sharon's academic journey reflects her dedication to continuous learning and excellence. She holds degrees from esteemed institutions such as Howard University, Walden University, Johns Hopkins University, National-Louis University, and Winston-Salem State University. Notably, she is an alumna of the 2019 Harvard University School of Education Women in Leadership Cohort, further solidifying her commitment to leadership development.

Acknowledged for her leadership acumen, Dr. Sharon is a proud member of the Forbes Coaches Council, International Association of Women (IAW), American Business Women's Association (ABWA), Black Women Educators Leaders (BWEL), Black Girls In Media (BGIM), National Association of Black Journalism (NABJ), and Delta Sigma Theta Sorority, Inc. Her influence extends to her role on the Board of Advisors for The Women of Prince George's, a testament to her dedication to the community and women's empowerment.

www.ingramcontent.com/pod-product-compliance
Lightning Source LLC
Chambersburg PA
CBHW051945160426
43198CB00013B/2315